TWAYNE'S WORLD AUTHORS SERIES

A Survey of the World's Literature

FRANCE

Maxwell A. Smith, Guerry Professor of French, Emeritus
The University of Chattanooga
Former Visiting Professor in Modern Languages
The Florida State University

EDITOR

Jean-Jacques Rousseau

TWAS 471

Jean-Jacques Rousseau

JEAN-JACQUES ROUSSEAU

By GEORGE R. HAVENS

The Ohio State University

TWAYNE PUBLISHERS

A DIVISION OF G. K. HALL & CO., BOSTON

Library of Congress Cataloging in Publication Data

Havens, George Remington, 1890–
    Jean-Jacques Rousseau.

    (Twayne's world authors series; TWAS 471: France)
    Bibliography pp. 131–35
    Includes index.
    1. Rousseau, Jean Jacques, 1712–1778—Biography.
2. Authors, French—18th century—Biography.
PQ2040.H38   848'.5'09   [B]   77–24169
ISBN 0–8057–6312–0

MANUFACTURED IN THE UNITED STATES OF AMERICA

To Paul M. Spurlin

Able scholar, firm friend

Contents

About the Author

George R. Havens, Professor Emeritus of French Literature at Ohio State University, received his B.A. degree at Amherst College and his Ph.D. at the Johns Hopkins University. He has taught also at Indiana University, and summers at Johns Hopkins, the University of Pennsylvania, Columbia, the University of Chicago (twice), and the University of California (Berkeley).

He is the author of *Selections from Voltaire,* the *Abbé Prévost and English Literature, Voltaire's Marginalia on Rousseau,* an edition of Voltaire's *Candide,* of Rousseau's *Discours sur les sciences et les arts,* of *Voltaire's Catalogue of his Library at Ferney* (with Professor Norman L. Torrey), of *Frederick J. Waugh: American Marine Painter,* and of the *Age of Ideas: From Reaction to Revolution in Eighteenth-Century France,* a book for the general reader as well as for the specialist.

Professor Havens made two trips to Leningrad (once as a Guggenheim Fellow) for study of Voltaire's books, purchased by Catherine the Great. He has resided several times in France and other European countries, doing research on Voltaire and Rousseau in libraries of Paris, London, Berlin, Geneva, and Neuchâtel. He is the author also of many articles, and the editor (with Donald F. Bond) of a *Critical Bibliography of French Literature in the Eighteenth Century,* the fourth volume in a series of which the general editor was David C. Cabeen.

A book in honor of Professor Havens, *Literature and History in the Age of Ideas,* edited by Charles G. S. Williams, was published by the Ohio State University Press in 1975. It contains articles by different authors in this country and abroad and also a bibliography of Professor Havens's writings.

Preface

In the eighteenth century Rousseau became a very controversial figure. He remains a strongly controversial figure today. Both his personality and his ideas sharply divided his contemporaries into enthusiastic friends or violent enemies. So it has often been with biographers or readers since his time. It has been well-nigh impossible, it seems, to be neutral, difficult to be fair and objective. Almost one can say that there have appeared to be as many different Rousseaus as writers about him.

Over the years, however, there have been notable exceptions to so sweeping a statement; and of late, particularly, much progress has been made in establishing the basic truth about Rousseau the man and Rousseau the writer. A major achievement is the new edition of his works, the *Œuvres complètes* in the Pléiade edition, Paris, Gallimard, edited by Bernard Gagnebin and Marcel Raymond with important contributions by other able Rousseau scholars. Of this admirable edition, four volumes of a projected five have so far appeared. They are on thin paper averaging well over 1900 pages for each compact and easily usable volume. The first volume dates from 1959, the second from 1961, the third from 1964, and the fourth from 1969. All are indexed except Volume II in which *La Nouvelle Héloïse* no doubt offered special difficulty.

Another major contribution in which we rejoice is the new critical edition of the Rousseau *Correspondance*, encouraged by the late Theodore Besterman and edited with excellent notes and admirable facsimiles by R. A. Leigh. The twenty-four volumes so far published, out of an estimated total of about forty, began to appear at Les Délices, Geneva, in 1965. The opening volume is adorned by an exceptional reproduction in color of the famous pastel of Rousseau by La Tour made in 1753, two years after the striking success of the First Discourse. This edition contains many newly-discovered letters by or to Rousseau and many letters more accurately reproduced directly from the original manuscripts tracked down from the various private or public collections scattered about the world. Coupled with the Gagnebin-Raymond edition of Rousseau's Works, this new edition of the *Correspondance* gives a much more complete and intimate picture of the personality, the development, and the ideas of Jean-Jacques than was ever possible before. It remains a major problem, however, to reflect accurately the huge mass of important material in these many volumes, so ably prepared and so rich in content.

The bibliography dealing with Rousseau has gradually risen over the years to several thousand books or articles. Some of these are indicated in the *Notes and References* or in the *Selected Bibliography* near the end of this volume.

It is not easy to do justice in brief space to a complex man like Rousseau. In French, there are many excellent discussions varying in length from three volumes to perhaps thirty pages—not so many, naturally, in English. There is need of such a discussion in English, fair, accurate, readable, and not too long. We have done our best to meet this need, difficult as we know it to be.

GEORGE R. HAVENS

Columbus, Ohio

Acknowledgments

To my good friends, Professors Charles G. S. Williams, Ralph E. Angelo, Walter Meiden, of the Ohio State University, Paul M. Spurlin of the University of Michigan, and Otis Fellows of Columbia University, I am indebted for numerous errands, bits of information, or occasional checking of data, which I was not in a position to do for myself. To them all, it is a special pleasure to express my warm appreciation and my heartfelt thanks.

Chronology

1712 June 28: Jean-Jacques Rousseau born in Geneva.

July 7: Death of Rousseau's mother, Suzanne Bernard Rousseau.

1722 October 3: Isaac Rousseau, Jean-Jacques's father, wounds Pierre Gautier, a retired army captain, with a sword.

October 11: Isaac Rousseau flees to Nyon, ten miles away, out of Genevan jurisdiction. Uncle Bernard promptly sends Jean-Jacques and cousin, Abraham Bernard, to board with a Protestant pastor, M. Lambercier, and his sister, Mlle Lambercier, at Bossey, a small village about four miles south of Geneva, under the government of Sardinia.

1724– Winter: Jean-Jacques returns to Geneva.
1725

1725 April 25: Uncle Bernard apprentices Jean-Jacques for five years to Abel Ducommun, a young master-engraver.

May 1: Jean-Jacques begins his apprenticeship with Ducommun.

1728 March 14, Sunday: Jean-Jacques, returning late from a tramp in the country, finds the gates of the walled city of Geneva closed, as usual, at sundown. Locked out for the night, he resolves not to return to Geneva to be beaten again by Ducommun.

March 21, Palm Sunday morning: Rousseau presents himself to Mme de Warens at Annecy in Savoy.

March 24: In the company of M. and Mme Sabran, Rousseau sets out on foot by the Mt. Cenis Pass over the Alps to Turin.

April 12: Rousseau is admitted to the monastery of the Spirito Santo in Turin to be converted to Catholicism.

April 21: Rousseau abjures Protestantism and becomes a Catholic.

July-part of August: Rousseau a vagabond in Turin.

August: Rousseau becomes a lackey of Mme de Vercellis.

September-October: Abbé Gaime talks to Rousseau about religion.

December 19: Rousseau's employment by Mme de Vercellis ended by her death. Marion and the stolen ribbon cause Rousseau remorse.

1729 January (?): Rousseau a privileged lackey of the Count de Gouvon. His son, the Abbé Gouvon, teaches Rousseau good Italian.

June (?): Rousseau returns to Mme de Warens at Annecy and begins to read widely. Abbé Gâtier supplements the religious influence of the Abbé Gaime, leading later to the *Vicaire savoyard* of *Emile* (1762).

1730 July 1: In an early morning walk, Rousseau meets Mlle Galley and Mlle de Graffenried, two girls of about his own age. Their all-day picnic together inspires the Julie and Claire of his novel, *La Nouvelle Héloïse*, twenty-six years later.

—— (?): Rousseau is publicly embarrassed when unable to direct an orchestra at the home of M. de Treytorens because of his inability to read music.

1731 April: Rousseau interpreter of the Reverend Father Athanasius Paulus, who claims to be Archimandrite of Jerusalem.

April: At Soleure the Marquis de Bonac, French ambassador, exposes the Archimandrite as an imposter, but gives Jean-Jacques one hundred francs to go to Paris.

June: Jean-Jacques makes this journey to Paris on foot in two weeks. His disappointment with his first impressions of poverty in Paris.

August: On his return trip, Rousseau stops for food and lodging at the home of a peasant and is struck with feelings of injustice and inequality at the peasant's fear of French taxes.

1732– Rousseau gives private lessons in music at Chambéry.
1733

1736– Rousseau's systematic study at Les Charmettes.
1740

Chronology

1739   Poem of the "Orchard of Mme de Warens" ("Le Verger de Mme de Warens").

1740–   Tutor of the two sons of M. de Mably at Lyons. "Project
1741   for the Education of M. de Sainte-Marie," the elder of the two boys.

1741   Rousseau's "Epistle to M. Borde."

1742   Rousseau's "Epistle to M. Parisot."
      August: Second trip to Paris. Rousseau presents his system of notation of music by numbers before the Academy of Sciences. Regarded as ingenious, but impractical.
      Daniel Roguin introduces Rousseau to Diderot.

1743   April: Rousseau frequents salon of Mme Dupin. Sees Voltaire there.

1743–   August 1743–August 1744: Secretary to M. de Montaigu,
1744   French ambassador at Venice.

1745   December 11: Rousseau's first letter to Voltaire.
      December 15: Voltaire's reply.

1745–   Beginnings of Rousseau's liaison with Thérèse Levasseur.
1746

1746–   Rousseau successively abandons his five children to the
1751   Foundling Asylum of Paris.

1749   October: *Le Mercure de France* announces a prize by the Academy of Dijon for a discourse on the beneficial effects of the Renaissance in man's knowledge.

1751   January 8: Probable date of publication of Rousseau's *Discourse on the Arts and Sciences.* (Cf. R. A. Leigh, *Corr. de Rousseau,* II, 135–36, n.1).

1751–   Rousseau's replies to refutations of his *Discourse.*
1753

1753   Autumn: Quarrel in Paris over Italian versus French music.
      October 17: Success of Rousseau's operetta, *The Village Soothsayer* (*Le Devin du village*), before the King and Court at Fontainebleau.
      November: *Le Mercure de France* announces a new prize by the Academy of Dijon on the origin of inequality among men.

1753–   Rousseau writes his *Discourse on Inequality* and submits
1754   it to the Academy of Dijon not later than April 1, 1754.

1754 July-September: Rousseau returns to Geneva, becomes again Protestant, and recovers his citizenship.

1755 August 20: Publication of the Second Discourse in Paris. August 30: Voltaire's famous letter attacking Rousseau's Second Discourse.
November: Rousseau's article on *Political Economy* appears in Vol. V of the *Encyclopedia*.

1756 April 9: Rousseau installed by Mme d'Epinay at the Hermitage.
August 18: Rousseau's letter to Voltaire on Providence. September 12: Voltaire's brief but courteous reply. Rousseau rewrites the Abbé de Saint-Pierre's *Essay on Polysynodie* and *Project for Perpetual Peace*. Rousseau working on his novel *La Nouvelle Héloïse, Emile,* and the *Social Contract*.

1757 October 10: Publication of Vol. VII of the *Encyclopedia* with its article on *Geneva* by d'Alembert.

1758 February-April: Rousseau writes his "Letter to d'Alembert on the theater."
Rousseau publishes his break with Diderot.

1758 October 2: Publication of the "Letter to d'Alembert."

1761 January 25: *La Nouvelle Héloïse* published in Paris.

1762 April: Publication of the *Social Contract*, but not permitted in Paris.
May 22: Mme de Luxembourg receives first copies of *Emile*.
June 8: Rousseau obliged to flee from Paris.
June 14: Rousseau arrives at Yverdon, in Bern, Switzerland.
June 29: *Emile* and the *Social Contract* burned in Geneva.
July 10: Rousseau, driven from Yverdon, goes to Môtiers, in the Val de Travers.
July 29: Death of Mme de Warens at Chambéry.
August 4: Rousseau makes declaration of faith in church of Pastor Montmollin at Môtiers.
August 28: Mandate of M. de Beaumont, Archbishop of Paris, issued against *Emile*.
September 4: Rousseau dons Armenian robe.

Chronology

1763   Rousseau's reply to M. de Beaumont published.

      May 12: Rousseau renounces his citizenship of Geneva.

1764   December 18: Rousseau's *Letters from the Mountain* reach Geneva.

      December 27: Voltaire publishes the anonymous *Opinion of the Citizens,* revealing Rousseau's abandonment of his children. Rousseau attributes the work mistakenly to Jacob Vernes, Genevan pastor.

      December 31: Rousseau receives the *Opinion of the Citizens.*

1764–   Either at the end of 1764 or beginning of 1765 Rousseau

1765   writes a first introduction to his *Confessions.*

1765   March 18: Rousseau begins his *Confessions.*

      Early July: Rousseau passes ten days on Ile de Saint-Pierre in Lake Bienne, Switzerland.

      September 6: Rousseau's house at Môtiers is stoned.

      September 12: Rousseau finds refuge on Ile de Saint-Pierre in territory of Bern. Forced to leave, Oct. 25.

      November 30: Rousseau decides to go to England with David Hume.

      December 16: Rousseau arrives in Paris.

      December 20: Housed by the Prince de Conti at the Temple.

1766   January 13: Rousseau and Hume arrive in London.

      March 19: Rousseau and Thérèse leave London for Wootten in Straffordshire. Rousseau writes five books of the *Confessions* at Wootten.

1767   March 18: King of England, George III, grants Rousseau a pension of 100 £. sterling annually.

      May 1: Rousseau and Thérèse flee from Wootten.

      May 21: Rousseau and Thérèse embark at Dover for Calais.

      June 21: Rousseau and Thérèse installed by Prince de Conti at Trye.

1768   January 3: Rousseau leaves Trye.

      June 18: Rousseau at Lyons.

      July 11: Rousseau at Grenoble.

      August 30: Rousseau marries Thérèse in an extralegal civil marriage at Bourgoin.

1769   November 15: Rousseau at Monquin writes Books VII-XI and all or part of Book XII of the *Confessions*.

1770   February 26: Long autobiographical letter of Rousseau to M. de Saint-Germain.

June: Rousseau returns to Paris, Rue Plâtrière, Hôtel du Saint-Espirit, then furnishes an apartment on the 6th floor in the Rue Plâtrière.

June 2: Rousseau subscribes to a statue of Voltaire.

June 17: Rousseau visits Buffon at Montbard.

December: Rousseau probably completes his *Confessions*, Book XII (but cf. November, 1769).

1771   February and May: Rousseau reads parts of his *Confessions* to audiences in Paris. (June, 1772, according to Bernardin de Saint-Pierre).

1772   Rousseau begins his *Dialogues, Rousseau juge de Jean-Jacques*.

1774   December: Rousseau moves to a lower floor, Rue Plâtrière.

1776   February 24: Rousseau finds gates of the altar closed at the cathedral of Notre-Dame-de-Paris and is unable to leave the manuscript of his *Dialogues* there.

February 25: Rousseau gives the manuscript of his *Dialogues* to Condillac for safekeeping.

Autumn: Rousseau composes the first *Walk* (*Promenade*) of his *Reveries*.

October 24: Returning from a walk, Rousseau is accidentally knocked down by a big dog, lies unconscious, but recovers and walks home to Rue Plâtrière.

December: False report of Rousseau's death.

1777   Winter to Summer: Rousseau composes second, third, fourth, fifth, sixth, and seventh *Walks* of his *Reveries*.

1778   End of Winter: Rousseau composes his eighth *Walk*.

March: Rousseau composes his ninth *Walk*.

April 12, Palm Sunday: Fiftieth anniversary of his first meeting with Mme de Warens at Annecy, Rousseau composes his tenth and last *Walk*, left unfinished.

May 2: Rousseau in Paris deposits manuscript copies of his *Confessions* and of his *Dialogues* with his old friend Paul Moultou, of Geneva.

May 20: Rousseau accepts the invitation of the Marquis

René de Girardin to establish himself at Ermenonville, the Marquis's country estate north of Paris.

June: Rousseau botanizes in the vicinity of Ermenonville, often in the company of the second son of the Marquis de Girardin.

July 2: Rousseau, as usual, rises with the sun at 5:00 A.M. and goes for a walk in the countryside. At 7:00 A.M. he breakfasts with Thérèse and a servant on a cup of coffee with milk. Taken suddenly ill, he collapses, and dies at 11:00 A.M., only a little over a month later than Voltaire, who had died in Paris on May 30; but Rousseau, at sixty-six, was eighteen years younger than Voltaire.

July 3: Sculptor Houdon makes death mask of Rousseau.

July 4: Rousseau buried in the Island of Poplars, near Ermenonville, at 11:00 at night.

1782   July: Publication of the first six books of the *Confessions* with the *Reveries*.

1789   November: Publication of the last six books of the *Confessions*.

1794   October 11: Transfer of the remains of Rousseau to the Pantheon of Paris, where those of Voltaire had been deposited in 1791.

CHAPTER 1

Rousseau's First Years (1712-1749)

JEAN-Jacques Rousseau was born in Geneva on June 28, 1712, the son of a watchmaker, Isaac Rousseau, and his wife, *née* Suzanne Bernard. Both parents belonged to the lower bourgeoisie or middle class and both enjoyed the distinctly minority privilege of being classed among the citizens of this thriving Protestant city, surrounded by strong Catholic rivals, France, Savoy, and the territory ruled by the king of Sardinia.

I Early Life at Geneva and Bossey

Rousseau was born in a house located at No. 40 of today's Grand' Rue, which climbs steeply up the hill from the left bank of the Rhone toward the Hôtel de Ville and the ancient twelfth-century Cathedral of Saint-Pierre. This was the older part of the historic city.

Geneva, the city of Calvin, still remained in the eighteenth century very much of a Protestant stronghold, opposed to the establishment of a theater, forbidding by law all luxury and indulgence in fine clothes, regulating morals. Indeed, even the use of vehicles was prohibited within the city, noted the visiting d'Alembert in 1756-1757.[1] People moved about the streets quietly on foot. Only a gradual increase in wealth and the presence of a traveled aristocracy, familiar with Paris and the outside world, tended to weaken among the upper classes Geneva's fond look back toward a more austere past. Yet this walled city continued to close its gates at sundown for nighttime protection against neighboring enemies and kept heavy chains stretched across the Rhone at its entrance from Lake Geneva to block attack from that quarter. The people still took legitimate pride in having repelled the sudden treacherous attempt at invasion by the Duke of Savoy with troops using lad-

21

ders to scale the walls. This was the famous "Escalade" on the night of December 11–12, 1602. The annual celebration of such a great defensive victory intensified the city's proud patriotism. The population of Geneva in the early part of the eighteenth century numbered about 18,500.[2] It was divided into four distinct categories known as Subjects, Inhabitants, Natives, and finally Citizens. Only male *citizens* of twenty-five years of age or over possessed the privilege of the vote. Of these citizens, casting their ballots in quiet, orderly fashion in the centrally-located Cathedral of Saint-Pierre,[3] there were at this time some 1,500. To be a "Citizen" was therefore a distinction belonging to only a small minority of the total population. Thus Rousseau had good reason to use the term "Citizen of Geneva" as a proud expression of rank which could not apply to mere subjects of the King of France or of other countries living under an absolute form of government without the vote.

Yet in reality Geneva was far less democratic than it seemed at first to Rousseau. The Grand Council of the whole body of 1,500 citizens, while it did exercise voting rights, wielded little actual power. It was indeed permitted to elect a Council of Two Hundred, and this organization in turn chose the members of an Executive Council of Twenty-five, but the nominations remained in the hands of these two much smaller bodies, which thus became readily self-perpetuating. In short, an aristocratic group of the "first families," contemptuous of prevailing austerity and sumptuary laws as far as they themselves were concerned, maintained its own autocratic rule. Rousseau was slow to perceive these realities of government in his native city which, as we shall see, he so early abandoned.

Jean-Jacques never knew his mother who died nine days later of fever resulting from his birth. Consequently he was brought up in his first years by a father who was himself largely undisciplined. The boy learned to read precociously, absorbed by the wildly romantic novels which he found at hand in his mother's library. Repeatedly he sat up reading late into the night with his father until finally the latter, shamefacedly, packed them both off to bed, exclaiming: "I'm more of a child than you are!" These novels filled the boy's mind with a totally unrealistic picture of life, which dominated his early years, but perhaps saved him from complete despair in face of the many grave misfortunes which befell him.

After the novels, however, came more serious reading, books chosen from the ministerial library of Rousseau's maternal grandfather. These were historians and moralists, above all the famous Greek biographer Plutarch ably translated into sixteenth-century French by Amyot. Jean-Jacques devoured Plutarch eagerly, captivated by the heroes of ancient Greece and Rome, and inspired to imitate, in imagination at least, their civic and patriotic virtues. In fact, Plutarch remained one of his favorite authors throughout his life. Another source of inspiration was the great sixteenth-century French essayist Montaigne, who became a strong motive force later behind Rousseau's *Confessions,* which are much franker, however, than those of his predecessor who, Jean-Jacques maintained, confessed only his more amiable weaknesses. Often too his father talked to the boy sentimentally about his departed mother, the two weeping together over these half-embroidered memories of the past.

After five years in Rousseau's birthplace on the Grand' Rue high up the hill in the older part of the city, the father sold the house he had inherited there and moved in June of 1717 (*OC,* Pléiade ed., I, 6, n. 1) to the new lower part of Geneva in the Saint-Gervais Quarter on the opposite bank of the swift-flowing Rhone. Here he settled with his young son and Rousseau's older scapegrace brother at what is today's No. 28 in the former Rue Coutance, now appropriately renamed Rue Jean-Jacques Rousseau. In this second home the family stayed for another five years until October of 1722 when the hot-tempered father got into a public quarrel and with a sword wounded his adversary, a retired army captain named Pierre Gautier. Faced with prompt imprisonment, the elder Rousseau hastily decamped to Nyon, some ten miles east on the northern shore of Lake Geneva. Here he was safe under another jurisdiction. It was characteristic of him that he found no difficulty in leaving his ten-year-old younger son behind in the care of the boy's Uncle Bernard. The latter in turn soon sent Jean-Jacques and his cousin of similar age to board with a Protestant pastor and his sister, M. and Mlle Lambercier, at Bossey. This was a pleasant country village nestled close beneath the foot of the

steep-rising granite barrier of the Salève only three or four miles
south of Geneva, but under the rule of the king of Sardinia.

At Bossey with his cousin, Abraham Bernard, the boy Rousseau spent two years or a little more, years which lingered
in his mind as nearly idyllic. He delighted in long walks
through this beautiful countryside, drank in the good pastor's
daily readings aloud from the Bible in family worship, and
attended services in the Protestant temple on Sundays. There
he was imbued for life with the sonorous Biblical phrases and
their bold oriental imagery and received a deep imprint from the
sermons heard in church. He even aspired to preach himself,
remembering the moral teachings of the pastor and his sister,
and to some degree absorbed the much-needed discipline
which, belatedly in the absence of his careless father at Nyon,
they tried their best to give him. On the other hand, two well-
deserved spankings by Mlle Lambercier, instead of their intended effect of punishment, stirred in him a latent masochistic
feeling of sexual pleasure which the pastor's sister, quickly per-
ceiving, wisely decided not to repeat. As a first experience of injustice, however, the boy never, over the long years, forgot having been falsely accused and most painfully punished by Uncle
Bernard for allegedly breaking a comb belonging to Mlle
Lambercier. Appearances were so strongly against him that
his firm denials, maintained long after the event itself, were of
no avail. Slight though the incident was, this deep conviction of
having suffered a grave injustice remained with him when he
told it long afterwards in his *Confessions*. It was an event that
tarnished his otherwise happy recollections of Bossey, offering
a striking example of how deep-rooted can be the memories
of childhood.

In contrast, Rousseau took an obvious pleasure later in narrating with a decidedly humorous touch M. Lambercier's solemn
planting of a walnut tree. The whole affair was attended with
such ceremony that Jean-Jacques and his cousin, deeply im-
pressed, concluded in their turn that they could do no less
than set out for themselves a shoot of willow. Slyly they dug
a trench leading from M. Lambercier's august tree, worked
hard to get the right slope, covered the trench over carefully
to conceal it, then looked on happily while the water drained

down to their slight willow as M. Lambercier each day poured it at the foot of his own walnut. But, in their childish delight, the two children could not refrain from shouts of triumph which quickly betrayed their secret.

"An aqueduct, an aqueduct!" cried M. Lambercier in amazement as he trampled their carefully-dug trench into oblivion.

But the pastor made no further mention of the incident, inflicted no additional punishment. So it was that Rousseau remembered the whole experience with pleasure and related it in detail years later, not with disappointment or any feeling of small tragedy, as might have been expected, but humorously in terms of the mock-heroic. In fact, he always regretted that, when he returned briefly to Geneva in late summer of 1754 with the text of his *Discourse on Inequality,* he did not take time to visit Bossey again and observe the progress of M. Lambercier's cherished walnut tree, hallowed by more than thirty years of additional growth.

At some period about this time in Rousseau's boyhood he had an imagined love affair with a Mlle de Vulson who was a full ten years older than himself. What disillusionment when Jean-Jacques discovered that her visit to Geneva from nearby Nyon, supposedly to see him, had really been to buy a gown for her approaching wedding! Twenty years later on a visit to his father at his refuge in this same Nyon, they saw, during an outing on the lake, another boat coming toward them with a family party. "Who are those ladies?" inquired Rousseau curiously. "Doesn't your heart tell you?" replied his father with a smile. "That's one of your old loves. That's Mme Crispin, Mlle de Vulson she used to be." At this almost-forgotten name, Rousseau did not laugh. Instead, he promptly directed the oarsmen to change their course and avoid the other boat.

There was a kind of sequel to the spankings abandoned by Mlle Lambercier. A Mlle Goton, pert minx of Rousseau's own age, amused herself by playing the role of a stern schoolteacher spanking the submissive boy for his imagined derelictions as her pupil. These were punishments which Jean-Jacques once more perversely enjoyed, though other little girls, in on the ill-kept secret, taunted him in penetrating whispers as he walked along the Rue Coutance: "Goton spat, spat Rousseau!" ("Goton tic tac Rousseau.")

But the largely happy life at Bossey came, alas! to an end. Uncle Bernard, anxious to get Jean-Jacques off his hands after a few dragging months, set him to earning his own living as an assistant to the registrar of the district, a man named Masseron. Rousseau, however, still only twelve years old we must remember, showed a marked dislike for the law and all legal records. Through carelessness or plain inefficiency he soon worked himself out of this dull job, to the disillusion of all concerned. What now? Uncle Bernard did not give up. On April 26, 1728, he signed a formal contract making Jean-Jacques an apprentice for five years to a young master-engraver named Abel Ducommun.

By the terms of this contract Uncle Bernard agreed to pay three hundred silver livres in three installments at specified periods, plus a bonus on the first of August of two gold louis. He agreed further to provide for the boy's clothes and laundry. Ducommun, for his part, would furnish lodging and meals, except desserts, which were not given to apprentices. Ducommun promised to teach Rousseau as much of the art of engraving as the apprentice, with good will and application, might be able to learn, and engaged solemnly to bring him up "in the fear of God and to instruct him in good conduct, as befits the father of a family" (I, 1207–08).

Ducommun himself, however, at the youthful age of twenty, was only seven years older than Rousseau. Moreover, far from being the august "father of a family," ready to assume the serious responsibilities of such a station, Ducommun was not even married until the following year (I, 30, n. 4). That he was already a master-engraver, though so young, was no doubt a tribute to his hard work and intelligent application, but hardly aided him in comprehending the largely undisciplined boy of less than thirteen that Rousseau in the spring of 1725 still showed himself to be.

In his *Confessions* Jean-Jacques insists that basically he liked engraving and the use of engraving tools. This statement is confirmed by his later devotion to the beautifully handwritten book manuscripts which he labored over for months and gave to friends like Mme d'Houdetot and Mme de Luxembourg as well as the care with which he described in advance the engraved illustrations intended for his great novel, *La Nouvelle Héloïse* (*The New Heloïse*).

So the boy might indeed have aspired to perfecting himself in his new profession, but, alas! Ducommun's rough treatment and the tight rein with which he drove his apprentices was more than Jean-Jacques could endure. This experience was a painfully sharp contrast to the affectionate family life he had mainly found with M. and Mlle Lambercier. And to leave the table now in mid-meal, as it were, without dessert, seemed an added affront to a boy who already had and later retained a special pleasure in good eating. So he snitched little delicacies, tasty asparagus, an apple from the pantry, then gradually extended his thefts to engraving tools and designs locked up in Ducommun's cabinet. He even amused himself by engraving contraband medals for a kind of chivalric order thought up by Ducommun's band of refractory apprentices. Such transgressions brought him hard thrashings by his master, punishments which Rousseau came to take as a matter of course without being in any way reformed by them.

But Sundays in fine weather offered delightful afternoons of freedom. After required attendance at Protestant church in the morning, Rousseau would join his comrades in fleeing the weekly bondage, leaving the city behind him for the delight of long tramps in the beautiful Swiss countryside. Always extreme in whatever he did, Jean-Jacques was prone to go farther than the others. Twice he came back late to find the gates of the walled city closed as usual at sundown. Forced to remain out all night, he returned on Monday morning to the expected beating by his master. So he made up his mind that if he were locked out a third time, he would not come back again to Geneva. Knowing Rousseau, we can be sure that he would be locked out a third time, and so he was.

II   *Annecy and Turin*

In the middle of March, 1728, Rousseau was returning from one of his usual Sunday-afternoon excursions in the country. He was late again, or else, as he tells the story in his *Confessions*, a

certain Captain Minutoli, when he was on duty, took a malicious
pleasure in closing the gates a half-hour early. Dramatically,
Rousseau's narrative proceeds. There sounded on the bugle
the mournful strains of the retreat. He was still a half a league—
well over a mile—from the city. Next he heard the brisk roll
of the drums. Doubling his pace, he shouted to the soldiers on
guard, saw the drawbridge rise ominously in the air, threw himself down in pleading on the slope of the glacis. All in vain! The
gates would not open. He was once more locked out for the night.

Such a happening was in itself no great misfortune for Rousseau
in fine weather, but he was determined this time not to return
the next morning for another beating by his hated master. Instead, he would see what awaited him in the great world outside.

There appears to have been a steady business of conversion
to Catholicism of Protestant refugees from Geneva. Rousseau
no doubt was aware of this, may even have had overtures made
to him before. In any case, he seems to have had no great
hesitation as to what to do. After a few days of lodging and
pleasant eating with hospitable peasants in the neighborhood,
he made his way to Confignon six miles from Geneva and
sought out the aged priest there, M. de Pontverre. M. de Pontverre received the young fugitive well, talked to him earnestly of
the Protestant heresy, of the authority of Sacred Mother Church,
and entertained him with a good dinner. This last especially was
a convincing argument which Jean-Jacques, with the ready appetite of active boyhood, was in no mood to resist.

"Go to Annecy," M. de Pontverre advised him. "There you
will find a kind and charitable lady. A pension from the king of
Sardinia makes it possible for her to save other souls from
the Protestant error from which she has escaped herself" (*OC*,
I, 47).

For such charity Rousseau had no great enthusiasm. Still, there
was no other choice before him; so he set out light-heartedly
enough for Annecy. It was a journey he could easily have made—
though on foot—in a single day, but there was no hurry; so he
took three. Now it was that those romantic readings devoured
under flickering candlelight during the long evenings until late
at night with his father surged up again vividly in his mind.
Surely his own obvious merits would see him through whatever

might happen. Just a single castle would suffice for his modest ambition! There would be a lord and his lady, a love affair with a beautiful daughter, a close friend in her brother. All this his brilliant imagination held in store for him. What more could he wish? The reality over the next years was to be sadly different!

But at first it did not seem so as his shoes grated over the rough cobblestone streets of Annecy. It was Palm Sunday, March 21, 1728, just a week since the gates of Geneva had closed before him. Seeking out the address given him, he now first saw a lady about to enter the rear door of the church next to her home. He had expected with dull resignation to find a devout, elderly woman. Instead, here was the Mme de Warens to whom he had been sent, a beautiful woman in her barely twenty-nine years while he himself was still three months under sixteen. Surely a religion preached by a young, smiling, attractive woman like this could not fail to be true! Mme de Warens took the letter he had himself written with such boyish eloquence as he could command, read it through, and glanced hurriedly over the more conventional one from M. de Pontverre.

"Ah! my child, you are much too young to be running about the country like this. It's too bad! Go into the house and ask them to give you some breakfast while you're waiting for me. After mass, I'll come back and have a talk with you" (OC, I, 49).

At noon-day dinner, Mme de Warens listened attentively to his story. It was embellished no doubt with the romantic dreams of his boyhood, told with the ardor and unconscious art which already were beginning to be his when he was happy and at ease. But a scant three days later, provided with a minimum of money, Jean-Jacques set out in the doubtful company of a M. Sabran and his wife for Italy. The boy, in high spirits, felt himself to be a new Hannibal crossing the Alps. It must have been a hundred miles or more over the Mount Cenis pass to their destination, Turin. In his *Confessions,* Rousseau remembered the journey as one of only seven or eight days, but the pace had to be regulated by Mme Sabran's capacities. Just when Rousseau descended for the first time into the warm, smiling plains of northern Italy we do not know. The written records in any case prove that it was a full twenty days before he was registered as entering the monastery of the Spirito Santo at Turin. Certainly it seems hardly likely that, with no money left to Rousseau's name, with not even a change of clothes in his minimum baggage, M. and Mme Sabran would have kept his embarrassing presence on their hands a day longer than necessary.

It was April 12, 1728, when "Rosso, Gio Giaco, di Geneva" (I, 69, n.3,4,5), was registered as entering the monastery. The heavy door with its iron bars clanked ominously behind him and Jean-Jacques found himself facing a wooden altar surmounted by a crucifix. Looking around, he saw "four or five frightful bandits" (*OC* I, 60), as he called them in his *Confessions*, his prospective fellow converts. They had nothing better to do than to let themselves be reeducated in religion, under different names no doubt, as often as possible, lured by the hope of a few days with bed and board, followed by a meager collection of money at the end of the session. Through another iron door entered the women who were to be instructed, almost equally seedy in appearance. Suddenly, at this early age, Rousseau had confronting him a shocking first-hand vision of how the "other half" of society lives.

Not until the day after Rousseau had quitted Annecy did his father and Uncle Bernard take the trouble to follow him. Even then, on horseback as they were, they could easily have caught up with Jean-Jacques and his party, which was making its slow way on foot over the mountains, and have brought him back to his native Geneva. They made no effort to do so. It was evident they preferred to be rid of him. So they paid M. Ducommun an indemnity of twenty-five silver crowns "on the occasion of the desertion of Jean-Jacques, . . . son of the aforesaid Isaac," and his failure to return "within four months" to finish his apprenticeship. Such were the provisions of the new agreement drawn up on March 30, 1728, and signed by Isaac Rousseau, Abel Ducommun, and two witnesses before a notary (I, 1208–09).

Rousseau himself speculates that, if Ducommun had been older and wiser in dealing with him, he, Jean-Jacques, might never have left Geneva and might have continued a quiet and peaceful life as the simple artisan which he believed himself most fitted to be. Eugène Ritter and others have hazarded like guesses as to what might have been. Tempting as it is to speculate, we cannot rewrite history. It is difficult enough to tell it accurately as it was! Like Robert Frost, though the two were so different in other respects, Rousseau too might have said:

> Two roads diverged in a wood, and I—
> I took the one less traveled by,
> And that has made all the difference.

Jean-Jacques later came to be ashamed of his prompt conversion to Catholicism in the monastery of the Spirito Santo in Turin. In his *Confessions* he draws a picture of the young boy that he was, arguing for long days successfully against the priest in favor of Genevan Protestantism, quoting authorities from his abundant reading. The reality was of course quite different. Still under sixteen, unpracticed in debate, without money, and ignorant of where his next meal, once he was out of the monastery, could be coming from, he had no recourse but to make his abjuration within a few days just as the written record shows. He seems, however, to have been permitted to stay on for a time further in the monastery after his conversion. When he left the hospice, he had, according to the *Confessions,* twenty francs or the equivalent in Italian *lire* in his pocket. Other accounts say he had only a little over five francs. The larger sum appears more likely since he was able to subsist, if only in hand-to-mouth fashion, for several weeks in Turin without employment.

Still he enjoyed his new-found liberty to the full. With even a little money in his pocket, he felt rich and care-free for the time being. In a happy mood, he explored this Italian city, so different from the Puritan Geneva that he knew. Already he had picked up enough of the Piedmontese dialect to get along. The King of Sardinia had the best symphony orchestra in Europe at the time, according to the *Confessions,* and every morning Jean-Jacques delighted in listening to the royal mass. He found shelter with other homeless wanderers like himself in the house of a soldier's wife where he was fortunately able to locate a vacant pallet on the floor. True, they were all, family and strangers, crowded together in a single room; but it cost only a penny a night, and it was better than the streets. For a mere six or seven cents, he could get a meal of milk, cheese, eggs, and salad at a restaurant he knew. Spiced with a boy's ready appetite, such a meal seemed quite the equal of what he came to buy for six or seven francs years later. Still his meager twenty *lire* would not last forever. He must find work. But what could he do? He did a little minor engraving, but he had not progressed far enough to compete with the few master-engravers of Turin.

Luckily the kindly Mme Basile with whom he had lodged at last found him a place as a lackey in the service of the Comtesse de Vercellis. Rousseau's position with Mme de Vercellis was not unpleasant. The Comtesse spoke and wrote an excellent French. Jean-Jacques surmised that she was not Piedmontese, but of Savoyard origin, and this proved in fact to be the case. Afflicted with breast cancer, Mme de Vercellis found comfort in writing frequent letters; but since her doctor thought the actual writing too fatiguing for her, she took advantage of Rousseau's presence to dictate these letters to him. Though still only a boy of sixteen, he was already beginning to acquire some elementary notions of language and style. This association with Mme de Vercellis was therefore a godsend for him. He also wrote to Mme de Warens, letters which Mme de Vercellis enjoyed reading, but, though she questioned him and drew him out to a certain extent, it was always coldly, says Jean-Jacques, and he replied with a certain protective reserve.

Mme de Vercellis died, however, December 19, 1728 (I, 83, n. 3), terminating Rousseau's employment. Unfortunately, Rousseau's stay with her ended in a strange act which became for him one of the most painful of his confessions. Unaccountably, he stole a small strip of ribbon, rose and silver in color, and already worn. Questioned, in sudden embarrassment he asserted it had been given him by a young girl, Marion, Mme de Vercellis's cook. Marion of course denied it and reproached Rousseau for the lie, but Jean-Jacques was so insistent that people tended to believe him rather than the unlucky girl. Rousseau never forgot the incident, and always wondered bitterly what sad fate he might perhaps have inflicted on his victim. Why had he taken this pitiful piece of ribbon? Why had he lied about it? Why had he put the blame on Marion? He never knew. Taking the ribbon was a thoughtless mad impulse. Lying about it was an instinctive act of self-preservation. But he could never afterward erase the affair from his mind.

Now Rousseau was again at sea. Among acquaintances he had recently made was a Savoyard priest, thirty-seven years of age, the Abbé Gaime. The Abbé had spoken frankly to Rousseau about the boy's character and talents, drawing for him a realistic picture of life, a picture of which the romantic Jean-Jacques had much need. Gradually, too, the priest came around to the subject of religion. Though the Abbé necessarily spoke with caution, his ideas to a great extent formed the basis of what later became Rousseau's famous "Profession of Faith of the Savoyard Vicar," a challenging and for Rousseau a dangerously unorthodox part of his great educational novel, *Emile* (1762).

After having neglected Rousseau for five or six weeks, it seemed, the Count de la Roque, nephew of Mme de Vercellis and executor of her estate, came to tell him of a promising opportunity in the employ of a Count de Gouvon, a distinguished nobleman of the house of Solar. Rousseau, when interviewed, made a good impression on the Count de Gouvon through the sincerity of his replies to questioning. The Count in turn introduced Rousseau to his daughter-in-law, the Marquise de Breil, and to his son, the Abbé de Gouvon. Their attitude appeared of good augury to Rousseau, as in fact it was. They were treating him with more ceremony than a mere servant. He was indeed expected to wait on table, but he was not made to wear livery. Except for taking the dictation of a few letters, itself something of a distinction, as it had been with Mme de Vercellis, he was left quite free between meals.

One day while he was waiting on table, however, an incident occurred which turned all eyes on Rousseau. The House of Solar had on its coat of arms a device reading: "Tel fiert qui ne tue pas." The Piedmontese who were present, not strong in French, thought the *t* a mistake. They said the word should read *fier*, proud. The Count de Gouvon was about to answer when, seeing a look of comprehension flash over Rousseau's face, he called on him to reply. Jean-Jacques spoke up, explaining that *fiert* with the *t* was an Old French word derived from the Latin *ferit*, strikes, not from *ferus*, proud. Thus the motto should be translated: "There is one who strikes, but does not kill."

It was a grand moment for the youthful Rousseau. All eyes turned upon him in astonishment. Here was no simple lackey. Even the dark-haired Mlle de Breil of about Rousseau's own age, whom he secretly so much admired, showed appreciation of his triumph.

After this momentous dinner, the Count de Gouvon called Rousseau in, talked with him a full half-hour, and advised him to devote himself to the Count's son, the Abbé de Gouvon. The next day, the Abbé set out to help Rousseau improve the little Latin he already knew. He also taught him to read more slowly and thoughtfully instead of in the indiscriminate haste with which he had plunged into the miscellaneous books, good, bad, and indifferent, he had rented from the lending library of La Tribu back in Geneva.

The Abbé de Gouvon himself had been well educated at the University of Sienna. Very much a purist in language, he was more interested in good literature than in theology. Every morning now Rousseau spent writing at the dictation of the Abbé. Thus Jean-Jacques's position as a kind of secretary was more to his own advantage than to that of his kind mentor. The Abbé spent more time on his pupil than on his own concerns. From him Rousseau learned a pure Italian rather than the prevailing Piedmontese he heard around him, and he laid the basis for an improved taste in literature which proved of great help to him later when he came to study wholly by himself. Here he saw a promising future ahead of him. Surrounded by esteem, he enjoyed an opportunity to go ahead in every way possible.

But, as he himself confessed, the boy still cherished a crazy ambition to seek his fortune through sudden adventure. Enchanted with a young Genevan of his own age named Bâcle, Jean-Jacques could not rest content with the calm, purposeful life and prospects of the Gouvon household. Instead, he must needs throw all this to the dogs and return to Savoy with companion Bâcle. The two would work their way, as they imagined, exhibiting the Heron fountain which had been given to Jean-Jacques by the Count de Gouvon.

However, in order to learn any meaningful amount of

Italian from the Abbé de Gouvon, it has been reasoned, Rousseau must have remained in this hospitable household for several months. This would have taken him well into the year 1729.

III   *Annecy, Lausanne, Neuchâtel and Paris*

Moreover, returning to Annecy by the Mount Cenis pass, he would have been obliged to wait for the melting of the late winter and early spring snows. Thus we are led to the conclusion that he could hardly have reached Annecy before June at the earliest (I, 103, n.). There, waving a cold goodbye to his companion Bâcle, with whom he had so recently been inseparable, Jean-Jacques entered the house of Mme de Warens, his heart beating furiously, his legs trembling under him, his eyes barely seeing where he was going. Hardly surprised at his unannounced return, Mme de Warens welcomed him in matter-of-fact fashion.

"Poor boy! So here you are again! I knew you were too young for the journey to Italy. At any rate, I'm glad it didn't turn out as bad for you as I feared" (OC, I, 104).

From the window of the second-story room that was given him, Rousseau looked out with delight on a wide view of a small stream, attractive lawns, and an extensive countryside beyond. It was the first time he had seen green beneath his windows since those happy days at Bossey with M. and Mlle Lambercier. Keeping records for Mme de Warens, transcribing recipes, working with the herbs and drugs which were her pet experiments, Rousseau tells us he passed his time most enjoyably doing the things that interested him the least, all because he was doing them for Mme de Warens.

But, happily for him, that was not all he did. He began to read again. There were the *Spectator Papers* of Addison and Steele translated from the English. There were the political theorist Puffendorf, the free-thinking seventeenth-century French essayist Saint-Evremond, exiled in England. There was Voltaire's epic poem on Henry IV, the famous *Henriade,* so popular in the eighteenth century, so rarely read today. The *Spectator* especially, with its varied comments on all sorts of subjects, set Rousseau to thinking for himself, as the Abbé de Gouvon had encouraged him to do. For the first time, Jean-Jacques began to distinguish between the provincial expressions he had learned in Geneva and the purer French of France. Reading the *Henriade*, he corrected his spelling and added a circumflex accent to the third person singular of the imperfect subjunctive. Sometimes he read aloud to Mme de Warens and discussed his reading with her. She had acquired a certain good taste in literature which she now passed along to the youthful Jean-Jacques. They read together the seventeenth-century La Bruyère with his varied criticisms of man and society. Mme de Warens preferred La Bruyère to his contemporary, the "sad and pessimistic" La Rochefoucald, as she described him, so disillusioning to the romantic notions of the Rousseau of these early days.

During all this time, Mme de Warens was secretly observing Rousseau, trying to uncover any latent possibilities. There was evident a sharp contrast between his ardent, passionate temperament, and the slow embarrassed manner in which he formed and expressed his ideas. He might well have been two different persons in one, he imagined, as he looked back on himself in his *Confessions*. From this slowness of thought and expression, he reflected, came the great difficulty he found in writing and the many revisions necessary before he could attain the final form toward which he worked so painfully.

For a time he studied in the nearby seminary, but neither his meager Latin nor his limited abilities, it was finally decided, would let him become even a country priest. He was beginning, however, to show a taste for music. Mme de Warens, his dear "mother," as he affectionately called her, had taught him something of singing while accompanying him on her harpsichord.

But there was one positive result from his brief stay in the seminary. He had met there an Abbé Gâtier, only twenty-six years old, who, supplementing the ideas and counsel of the Abbé Gaime, whom he had known at Turin, helped Rousseau further on his way toward the religious ideas expressed more than thirty years later by the Savoyard Vicar in *Emile*.

One Sunday a fire broke out in the church next door. Only a sudden change in the wind saved the house of Mme de Warens. Young Jean-Jacques wrote and signed a statement confirming this "miracle," a document which, unearthed by the antiphilosophic journalist Fréron, came back to plague Rousseau many years afterwards when his rationalism was much more to the fore.

On an early morning at the beginning of July, 1730, Rousseau set out for one of his characteristic walks in the country. As he swung vigorously along enjoying the sunrise, the singing of the birds, and all aspects of this bright summer morning he heard behind him the rhythmic thump of horses' hoofs and the high staccato of girls' voices. The girls turned out to be acquaintances, a Mlle de Graffenried and a Mlle Galley, both only slightly different in age from Rousseau (I, 135, n. 2 and 3).[4] They were embarrassed, however, because their horses balked at fording a small stream. Rousseau, taking the bridle of Mlle Galley's horse, led him easily across the brook, the water coming to Jean-Jacques's knees. The other horse with its rider followed docilely after. As Rousseau was then about to decamp, the two girls insisted on taking him prisoner, as they gaily put it. At their invitation, he mounted one of the horses behind Mlle de Graffenried, his arms timidly around her waist, though he could not avoid a flash of regret that he was not placed behind the blond Mlle Galley whom he considered more delicately beautiful. The two girls were on their way for a day's outing at the neighboring château of Thônes, or, as Rousseau put it in the local dialect, Toune. This was a medieval stronghold owned by Mlle Galley's widowed mother.

In the kitchen of the château, they all three had breakfast and later a picnic dinner together. After dinner, Rousseau climbed a nearby tree and playfully dropped down bunches of cherries by way of dessert, the two girls catching them in outstretched aprons. By chance, one bunch of cherries, missing the apron, fell into the neck of Mlle Galley's lowcut blouse as she leaned back. They all laughed heartily together, while Rousseau caught a fleeting glimpse of her breast.

On their return in late afternoon, the girls let Rousseau off at about the same place where he had joined them in early morning. From there he made his way back to Annecy. He never saw the two girls again, yet the day remained one of the deepest and happiest memories of his life.

More than twenty-five years later the details of this brief

experience surged up unexpectedly in his mind as, in his country Hermitage outside of Paris, Rousseau began to write the imagined letters which made up his great epistolary novel of *La Nouvelle Héloïse* (*The New Heloïse*). The blond Mlle Galley became his beloved heroine, Julie d'Etange, while the dark-haired Mlle de Graffenried was the model for her close friend and confidante, Claire d'Orbe.

Mme de Warens was off on a mysterious visit to Paris. Rousseau therefore decided to set out on a trip himself, accompanying one of the maids of the household, Anne-Marie Merceret, to her home at Fribourg, some seventy-five miles northeast of Annecy in Switzerland. On his way back, Rousseau, out of money, elected to stay for a while in Lausanne on the north shore of Lake Geneva in order to make a living, as he hoped, with music lessons.

Now comes one of the most remarkable of all the many stories told in Rousseau's *Confessions*. Jean-Jacques had become acquainted with a M. de Treytorens, Professor of Law, and ardent lover of music. Rousseau ambitiously decided to compose a piece for a concert at the professor's home and to direct the orchestra himself. An admirable idea, it seemed, except that he lacked all the necessary knowledge and ability to carry it out!

Nonetheless, after two weeks of busy preparation, Jean-Jacques stood solemnly before his musicians, called them to attention by tapping his baton on the desk in front of him, and began beating time. Alas! Unable as yet to read music from the notes, ignorant of the rules of composition, at a loss to know whether the members of his orchestra were playing their parts correctly or not, never, he writes, did anyone hear "such a chivaree" of discordant sounds. The worse the caterwauling, the more enthusiastically the musicians laid into their work. Poor Rousseau! Never had anyone been more publicly humiliated, and all because of his own mad impulse to do what he was in no way prepared to do. Who could have imagined, he muses in his *Confessions*, that on a later day his own operetta of the *Le Devin du village* (*Village Soothsayer*), would delight the gentlemen and ladies of the court of France including King Louis XV himself?

Adventure followed adventure! At a country inn near Neuchâtel, Rousseau met up with an impressive figure of a man with a long beard, fur cap, and purple robe, speaking a strange jargon of *lingua franca* mingled with bad Italian which Jean-Jacques, alone of those present, more or less understood. The stranger introduced himself as the Rev. Father Athanasius Paulus, Archimandrite or Abbot of the Greek Orthodox Church, engaged in soliciting funds for the restoration of the Holy Sepulcher at Jerusalem. Naturally Rousseau soon found himself installed as the official interpreter of the foreign priest, traveling comfortably with him about the country on horseback. Their dignity forbade them to beg from individuals. They would solicit only from government bodies. At Fribourg, results were mediocre; but before the Senate of Bern they did better, thanks to an impromptu speech by Rousseau who, on this occasion, surprisingly found himself able to speak for the Archimandrite as he could never do with assurance at a later date when only his own interests were involved.

But alas! at Soleure (or Solothurn) the Marquis de Bonac, French ambassador, familiar with Turkey and the Orient from long experience, quickly detected the Archimandrite as a rank imposter. By dint of recommendations obtained probably by Mme de Warens and supported also by some of his music pupils at Neuchâtel, (I, 158, n. 5), Rousseau, however, won aid from M. de Bonac, who gave him a hundred francs toward a journey to that Paris of which Jean-Jacques suddenly professed to be a native. The ambassador's secretary, in turn, facetiously challenged him as Rousseau the Second to equal the literary reputation of the poet Jean-Baptiste Rousseau whom he called Rousseau the First. Little did the good man dream that Rousseau the Second would one day far outstrip the fame of his predecessor.

It was a good three hundred miles overland to Paris, but Rousseau, vigorous walker that he was, took delight in such a voyage. The days are long in June and the chances of good weather excellent. What a pleasure for him, carefree for the moment, without encumbering baggage, to put one foot ahead of the other and swing along over the beautiful French countryside! Breathing deeply from exercise in the open air, he reveled in a keen sense of physical wellbeing. At the end of each day, he could look forward to a hearty dinner and a good night's sleep. This whole long journey was completed, he tells us, in about two weeks, but there was no reason for such a pace to tax him. All he had to do was to go along steadily at an average rate of about three miles an hour for some seven hours each day. There would still be time to stretch out occasionally by the roadside or to taste the luxury of rest for an hour or so before dinner at the end of each afternoon's march.

But there was unexpected disillusion at the completion of his journey. He had heard and read such striking reports of the grandeur and beauty of Paris. What expectations he had built up! The first contact with reality was quite different. As he walked into the city from the south, he saw only "the dirty, foul-smelling narrow streets of the Faubourg Saint-Marceau," the beggars, the dingy houses, the loud hawkers of cast-off wares, the teeming, jostling life of sordid poverty and filth. "This from the outset," he wrote later, "struck me so forcibly that all the real magnificence I have since found in Paris has been unable to wipe out my first impression, and I have always retained a secret dislike for residence in this capital" (OC, I, 159). Indeed, his whole experience in Paris was a disappointment. The city clearly offered no opportunity for this untrained boy to make his way there. After a few short weeks, he was glad by August to set out once more on the open road for Chambéry, Savoy and Mme de Warens.

IV   A Peasant and Taxes

On his return journey he had an unforgettable experience. Late one afternoon, losing his way, as he wandered in sight-seeing off the direct road, he ventured, dead-tired and raven-ously hungry, into the quite unattractive house of a peasant, the only choice available in this remote countryside. Rousseau asked if he could have dinner, saying he was ready to pay for it. Grudg-ingly, the peasant laid out for him some skim milk and a big loaf of barley bread, all he had, he declared (I, 164, n. 1,2,3,4).

But, when Jean-Jacques drank the milk and devoured the bread with obvious hunger, the peasant concluded that he was after all just what he said he was, a lone boy on his way home across the country. Thereupon the peasant lifted up a trap door in the floor next to the kitchen, went down into the basement, and shortly brought up a loaf of good whole-wheat bread, some appetizing ham, and a bottle of wine. To this he added a thick omelet, and Rousseau savored a dinner that stood out in his memory over the years. But when at length he made a movement to pay, the peasant again showed signs of unexplained uneasiness and fear. Jean-Jacques could not make out what was the matter with him as he heard his host uttering something about clerks and "cellar rats," whatever these last might be. It soon developed that he was in dread of a search by tax collectors, that he felt he would be an utterly ruined man unless he seemed on the point of dying from hunger. For the first time in his life Rousseau got a direct impression of the vicious eighteenth-century French system of farming out the taxes. He saw that they weighed most heavily on the lowest members of society, those least able to pay. It was an experience which tended to shape his whole future revolt against injustice.

This was the last of the long journeys Rousseau made on foot and he enjoyed it to the full, rejecting out of hand the urging to hire a horse for the ride home from Lyons. Always in the future he found that companions or the burden of baggage kept him from the fine freedom of these early years.

V *Mme de Warens*

Back once more in Chambéry by the end of September, 1732, Jean-Jacques gradually began making the rounds of private houses giving music lessons to girls in the region. The list of his students is long and imposing, but appears less impressive when we think of the lessons as coming no oftener than once a week, perhaps even at times only once in two weeks. But they were important. Rousseau learned music, he tells us, by teaching it.

Mme de Warens, however, feared he would be taken in by the wiles of these feminine pupils or of their intriguing mothers. Herself strangely amoral, she decided to protect him from outside influences by becoming his mistress. It was an unusual relationship for Rousseau, who still felt toward her as toward a mother. There was even a third member involved in Claude

Anet, who aided Mme de Warens in running her establishment at Chambéry. Anet died, however, in March 1734.

Gradually, as Rousseau drifted away from this intimacy with Mme de Warens, he began to realize that, at the approach of twenty-five, he was still woefully ignorant. So he began to work out for himself a plan of study and reading. Mathematics, science, philosophy, and Latin occupied his mornings; history, literature, and general reading he left as easier to the afternoons. Philosophy gave him particular trouble as he found each philosopher different from the rest, but no less confident of the truth of his own system. Finally, Jean-Jacques made up his mind to take each system as it came to hand, to try to understand it, and to form his own opinions only when he had a full basis for comparison.

This was a school in which Rousseau was both teacher and student. Evidently he lacked the advantage of a more informed and mature mind guiding his own. On the other hand, he was forced to develop his initiative and complete independence. He learned, moreover, in that best of all ways: because he wanted to learn, not because he was required to read or study. Each book that he took up became a new revelation and the reading of it stayed with him over the years. Chambéry and Les Charmettes, the charming country place nearby, became his private college. Here, to a great extent, he developed his character and his knowledge for life.

VI *Lyons, Paris again and Voltaire*

In 1740 Rousseau obtained a position at Lyons as tutor to the two young sons of a M. de Mably. It was a most important experience and he held the post for nearly a year, though he soon discovered himself too lacking in firmness and discipline to succeed as a teacher of these not easily manageable pupils. The task forced him, however, to reflect on the problems and goals of education. To this end, he drew up a "Project for the Education of M. de Sainte-Marie," the elder of the two boys. This essay is an important embodiment of his ideas, leading twenty years later to a more comprehensive treatise on education, his famous *Emile* (1762). Shaping the character, Rousseau concluded, is even more important than instructing the mind.

"Better a head well formed," he quoted from his favorite Montaigne, "than one well filled." It was a doctrine he had learned for himself through hard necessity.

Already in 1739, a year earlier, Rousseau had written a poem entitled *Le Verger de Mme de Warens* (*The Orchard of Mme de Warens*). Autobiographical, it evokes the author's delight in the charm and solitude of country living at Les Charmettes in the environs of Chambéry. Jean-Jacques gives expression to his stubborn independence and his refusal to court those patrons who might aid him in an upward push into society. The writer manifests also his well-known admiration for the supposed goodness of human nature and turns away from all writing which does not aim at the betterment of mankind. Thus early some of the most characteristic aspects of his later works begin to appear.

Rousseau had made two important friends at Lyons. One was a M. Borde, the other a surgeon, M. Parisot. Still experimenting with verse, Jean-Jacques wrote an *Epistle to M. Borde* and an *Epistle to M. Parisot.*

In his *Epistle to M. Borde* of 1741, new tendencies become evident. There is unexpected admiration for the luxury around him at Lyons, home of a thriving silk industry. This attitude is probably augmented by the impact of Voltaire's brief witty poem of "Le Mondain" ("The Mundane Man"), which had drawn so much public attention only a few years before in 1736, even involving its astonished author in attacks by the censorship and driving him into temporary exile outside of France. Rousseau tell us that in these early years he and Mme de Warens read everything published by Voltaire. It seems they could hardly have overlooked a poem so much in the public eye. In this admiration which Rousseau expresses for luxury there is already evident a sharp struggle between the austere simplicity of his Genevan heritage and a new note of modernism.

Likewise, in his *Epistle to M. Parisot* of 1742, the same contrast is revealed. Rousseau revolts against the great in society, yet, under urging from Mme de Warens, endeavors to be practical and to adapt himself to social demands, admiring "an illustrious nobility." Even the inequality seen about him has its justification, he thinks, in striking contrast to the *Discourse on the Origin of Inequality* which will come from his pen later in 1755. "Nothing should be carried to excess, not even virtue," he admits to Parisot, but he will not descend to intrigue or flattery in order to make his way in the world. He will seek happiness, but in pursuit of liberty and independence, not glory.

In these last three poems, Rousseau made a series of autobiographical "confessions." While expressing himself in verse, he was no doubt trying to emulate that "other" Rousseau, that Jean-Baptiste Rousseau who had preceded him in fame. No doubt too he felt inspired by the "master" of his early years, M. de Voltaire, who loomed before him as the great varied genius of his time. Later years would show that Jean-Jacques was in no way destined to become a poet, yet these early efforts at verse increased his vocabulary, gave him needed practice in the manipulation of language, taught him the many difficult problems of self-expression. Clearly they made a significant contribution to his development and offered an interesting revelation of his complex character.

Leaving now his friends in Lyons, Rousseau set out on a second voyage to Paris. This time he carried letters of introduction and a proposal for a new system of recording music by numbers instead of notes on a staff. It was August of 1742 (I, 282, n. 6). In contrast to his previous unfavorable impressions of the great city, almost everything he saw this time revealed the brilliant aspects of the capital. The only exception was the Hôtel Saint-Quentin in the Rue des Cordiers near the Sorbonne where he lodged on the recommendation of his friend Borde. "An ugly street, an ugly hotel, an ugly room," Rousseau observed succinctly in his *Confessions*. Still, distinguished men had stayed there, including not only his friend Borde, but the dramatist Gresset, the Abbé de Mably, the philosopher Condillac, and others. Rousseau met at the Hôtel Saint-Quentin a country squire named M. de Bonnefond, otherwise unknown to fame. M. de Bonnefond, however, introduced Rousseau to Daniel Roguin who in turn brought Jean-Jacques to the attention of Diderot. For fifteen years Diderot remained one of the closest of Rousseau's friends exerting an important influence on his literary work.

Carrying out his mission, Rousseau appeared before the Academy of Science in Paris and presented his system for writing down music. He was well received and met, among others, the distinguished entomologist, M. de Réaumur, known also for his famous thermometer. Rousseau's system was analyzed and received many compliments, but his proposal was not adopted. The great composer Rameau, as Rousseau observed, pointed out its chief defect. "Your signs," he said, "are very good. They indicate clearly the values, the length, and the intervals of the notes, better than the ordinary system, but they have one serious shortcoming. They require an operation of the mind which cannot always follow them with the rapidity needed for their execution. In contrast, the position of the notes on the staff reveals this instantly to the eye." Rousseau admitted the validity of this criticism which was unanswerable. He insisted, however, that he had used his system to teach music successfully in three months to "a young American," a French inhabitant of the West Indies, named Mlle Desroulins, who had been introduced to him by Daniel Roguin. Once more Rousseau was unable to convince others and his effort resulted in failure.

A happy development was his growing friendship with the philosopher Diderot in which their mutual interest in music formed an early bond between them. Daily, too, Jean-Jacques took a walk in the Paris Luxembourg Gardens, reading and endeavoring to memorize poems by Vergil or by Rousseau's famous predecessor, Jean-Baptiste Rousseau, who still seemed to be very much on his mind. Jean-Jacques also applied himself to the game of chess, fondly imagining that, by learning to outdo masters like Légal or Philidor, he could find another way of gaining the fame which so far had escaped him (I, 220–21 and n. 2).[5] This endeavor brought only further disappointment, naturally, but he did succeed in beating regularly the careless and impulsive Diderot, always refusing to favor his friend with an equalizing handicap.

In April of 1743, Père Castel introduced Rousseau into the circle of Mme Dupin (I, 288–93), wife of a wealthy tax farmer. There Rousseau saw, if mostly at a distance, a grand company of famous men and women whom she entertained in her salon or at dinner. Among them was the then eighty-six-year-old Fontenelle to whom Jean-Jacques had brought a letter of introduction and who was very kind to him. Of the company was the aged Abbé de Saint-Pierre, two of whose well-intended, but badly-written works, Rousseau was to revise and one of which he published later at the instance of Mme Dupin. Jean-Jacques also met the great naturalist Buffon, who gradually became a somewhat casual, but sincere friend. Voltaire was there too, but Rousseau did not dare approach him because of his own obscurity. Voltaire, however, probably did inform himself somewhat about Rousseau from Mme Dupin.

When did Voltaire in fact meet Rousseau? The famous proprietor of Les Délices wrote to Lieutenant-Colonel Charles Pictet about July 9, 1762: "I have seen only once in my life the individual Jean-Jacques Rousseau at Paris twenty-five years ago" (Leigh, XI, 258).

It has long been supposed that this meeting took place in the late winter or spring of 1750 through the good offices of Mme de Graffigny (I, 292, n.3). We now learn, however, that Mme de Graffigny did not herself know Rousseau in 1750. She first met him on October 28, 1751, as she states in her letter of the next day to Panpan Devaux at Lunéville: "Yesterday I made the acquaintance of that Rousseau who is becoming so celebrated through his paradox and through his reply to your king [Stanislas]."[6]

Now Voltaire, as we have just observed from the *Confessions* (I, 292), was one of the many distinguished guests at the salon and dinners of Mme Dupin in the spring of 1743, though Rousseau, not yet installed as her secretary, was too timid himself to seek out the celebrated poet and dramatist. It seems probable, however, that Voltaire could hardly have failed to see him there and that he obtained enough information from Mme Dupin to satisfy his bare minimum of curiosity about the obscure figure that Rousseau still remained at that time. Moreover, this occasion would have been nineteen years before the letter of 1762 to Pictet, much nearer the twenty-five-year figure so carelessly tossed out by the high and mighty Voltaire of that moment than the date of 1750 previously favored.

VII *Venice and the French Ambassador*

While in Paris during the late spring of 1743, Rousseau was suddenly engaged as secretary of a M. de Montaigu, ex-soldier and now French ambassador to Venice. This turn of affairs was surprising for Jean-Jacques, but seemed to offer a welcome opportunity. After a long journey in which he was delayed a month by quarantine for the plague at Genoa, he finally arrived at Venice in September, 1743. In the *Confessions* Rousseau recorded his stay in the diplomatic service as having lasted a year and a half. His memory played him false, however. The actual time spent in this Italian city was almost exactly one year. It was in September, 1744, that he left Venice after a violent quarrel for which both sides must bear their share of blame.

But at first all gave promise of unexpected success. Rousseau had the basic advantage of a good knowledge of Italian, a talent sadly lacking, it appears, to M. de Montaigu. Moreover, buttressed by a natural pride in representing a great country like France, Rousseau manifested on several occasions a courage and a firmness hardly to be expected from his previous experience. For the first time he was led to reflect on the influence exerted by the form and character of a government on the manners and morals of a people. These were ideas which resulted ultimately in a notable political work from his pen, his *Social Contract* of 1762.

In his relations with M. de Montaigu, however, Rousseau showed a stubborn neglect of tact. Far superior to his employer in his gift for literary expression, Jean-Jacques lolled at ease in the lone armchair he had deliberately selected for himself, ostentatiously reading a book, while waiting for the ambassador, M. de Montaigu, to find the halting words with which he dictated his blundering diplomatic letters. We have our knowledge of this surprising conduct on the admission of M. de Montaigu himself who could hardly have invented an incident so revealing of his own incapacity (I, 309, n.2). Finally there came a violent quarrel between these two unequal antagonists, and Rousseau, dismissed by his superior, made his way back to Paris. There he found that, whatever the merits of his grievances, a commoner against a nobleman had no redress. He did receive his back pay, but the rest of his experience left a festering wound in protest against the inequalities of society, a wound which, whatever the degree of his own responsibility, would not heal.

About this time Jean-Jacques entered into a sad liaison with a poor servant girl, Thérèse Levasseur, shockingly illiterate, completely incapable of entering into Rousseau's ideas or aspirations, in no way apt to share his changing moods. Yet during the next several years they had five children, all of them abandoned to the Paris foundling asylum where they disappeared forever. These children evoked a slowly developing remorse on the part of Rousseau, a remorse which never left him, but came to form a torturing background to his educational novel, *Emile* (1762), and to his posthumous *Confessions* (1782–1789).

Admitted to the circle of M. and Mme de La Popelinière, though certainly on no basis of equality, Rousseau must have caught glimpses there of the beauteous Mme d'Etioles who, in the spring of 1745, became through the favor of Louis XV, Mme de Pompadour (I, 334, n.3).

In December of this same 1745, Rousseau first entered into correspondence with that object of his youthful admiration, M. de Voltaire. The Duc de Richelieu, charged with providing court amusements for the King, called upon Rousseau to revise Voltaire's light theatrical piece, *The Princess of Navarre*, now rechristened *The Festivals of Ramire*, in order to adapt the words to the music of the famous composer Rameau. In a polite exchange of letters, Voltaire gracefully gave Rousseau permission to make any changes in the text he might find necessary. For Voltaire, the whole affair was of slight importance at this moment in his already brilliant career. To Rousseau, still obscure, but ambitious, such an assignment seemed to offer a promising step forward. In the end, however, he was keenly disappointed when his name did not appear on the program presented to the King.[7] Contrary to Rousseau's opinion in the *Confessions* (I, 338, n.3), Voltaire's name also did not appear on the program. Rousseau asserts that Voltaire was then in Lorraine [Cirey], but Besterman (Voltaire's *Corr.*, IX, 371, n.) says "both men were in Paris," a statement apparently confirmed by Voltaire's letters of this period. It is clear that Jean-Jacques did not receive his pay for the work he performed (*Confessions*, I, 338, n. 1 and 4).

For several years from about 1745 until after the great success of the First Discourse in 1751, Rousseau served as secretary to Mme Dupin (I, 292, n.1,2,3,4). Among his duties figured research for her undistinguished literary efforts and the preparation of clear copies for publication. It was boring work, intensified by the fact that Mme Dupin, though kind enough in her treatment of him, quite failed to perceive Jean-Jacques's own developing gifts and was utterly surprised when Rousseau suddenly rose to fame (I, 116–17, 341–42).

CHAPTER 2

Rousseau's Rise to Fame (1749–1758)

I Diderot Imprisoned

ON July 24, 1749, Rousseau's closest friend, Diderot, was suddenly arrested by the French government for the boldness of his philosophical works and—the Bastille being full—he was hurried off to prison high up in the towering Donjon of Vincennes a few miles east of Paris. Jean-Jacques was in despair. With his natural pessimism, he feared that Diderot was jailed for life. Not knowing what else to do, he ventured to write the King's mistress, Mme de Pompadour, whom he had seen casually in the circle of M. and Mme de La Popelinière four or five years before when she was still known only as Mme d'Etioles. He received no answer. His letter, he admitted, was too wild in content to have any effect.

At first Diderot boldly denied all charges. Solitary confinement, however, was especially painful to a man of his expansive and talkative nature. After a month, with no hope of release otherwise, he was constrained to admit authorship of the forbidden works and to promise good behavior in the future. In return for his humble admission, he was transferred from the Donjon to the neighboring château with permission, on his parole not to escape, to take walks in the adjacent unwalled grounds and to receive visits from his friends.

On August 25, therefore, after a delay of two or three days because of necessary work for Mme Dupin, Rousseau hastened out to see Diderot at Vincennes. He found d'Alembert, Diderot's associate as director of the great *Encyclopedia*, already there before him. Diderot appeared much worn down by his imprisonment. Nearly every other day Rousseau made the journey to Vincennes from his solitary room in central Paris near the Louvre and the Palais-Royal, then the seat of the Opera. When-

50

ever he did not accompany Mme Diderot in an expensive cab, he accomplished the twelve-mile round trip on foot. Impatient to arrive, Jean-Jacques was inclined to set too fast a pace for the heat of summer, prolonged, as it so frequently is, into the fall. As a consequence, he often reached his destination dead-tired and all-of-a-sweat with exhaustion. To moderate this hurried pace, he hit on the idea of taking with him something to read. Then, throwing himself down by the side of the road, he could profit from a needed rest from time to time on the way.

II *Rousseau's First Discourse (1751)*

One afternoon on this road to Vincennes, looking through the recently-published October number of the famous monthly magazine, *Le Mercure de France*,[1] Rousseau's eyes fell suddenly on the announcement of a prize contest offered by the Academy of Dijon for the best essay on the subject: "Did the Renaissance in the Arts and Sciences Contribute to Purifying Morals?" Each essay, limited to what could be read in a half-hour, was to be submitted to the Academy no later than April 1, 1750.

At once Rousseau took fire. Sharpening the question by inserting after the word "purifying" the contrasting phrase "or to corrupting," he chose the negative answer and, pulling a pencil from his pocket, began to write the famous apostrophe to the Roman Fabricius which went later into the middle of his Discourse.

Arrived at Vincennes, Rousseau read to Diderot what he had written and talked to him about the subject. There has been controversy as to whether Jean-Jacques had not first contemplated taking the affirmative side of the question, only to be persuaded in the end by Diderot to choose the negative as the more striking and more challenging position. Such a claim seems most unlikely. Diderot himself does not go so far. He declares simply that Rousseau took the side more natural to him, the side in harmony with his increasing criticism of society over the years. The negative was also in accord with the apostrophe to Fabricius just written at white heat by the roadside. No doubt Diderot himself, after his irksome confinement in the

Donjon, was ready enough to encourage Rousseau strongly in the negative, no doubt he offered many suggestions, came almost at times, as his habit was, to act as though he had composed the Discourse himself.

Gradually Rousseau completed his essay, rounding out his sentences during his many sleepless nights, then dictating them from bed in the morning to the mother of Thérèse, Mme Levasseur, who came early to start his fire, straighten out his room, and prepare his light breakfast. Mme Levasseur was not quite as illiterate as her unfortunate daughter. Still a brief example of her work preserved in the Rousseau archives at Neuchâtel exhibits a French spelling which was very much her own. Rousseau, however, happy to take advantage of her aid, transcribed her notes without comment on their form.

Jean-Jacques sent off his essay to Dijon before the required deadline of April 1, 1750, though with little hope of success after the many disappointments he had already experienced. On Friday, July 10, not July 9, as recorded by mistake in the Academy's minutes, the first prize was awarded to Rousseau. A week or so later Jean-Jacques received by mail the unexpected news from Dijon and on Monday, July 20, in his most careful handwriting, sent a brief letter of acceptance to the Academicians. The actual public award was made, as had been prearranged, on Sunday, August, 23, the author himself remaining absent in Paris. His Discourse was, however, read aloud to the audience by the Secretary, Claude Gelot.

During the closing weeks of autumn, while Rousseau was ill in bed with a severe case of nephritis, Diderot, already known in literary circles, secured him a publisher, the Parisian Pissot. There was little confidence, however, in any great reader demand for such a prize discourse; therefore publication was arranged for without royalties. As Rousseau said later, "I never received a penny for my Discourse."

Le Mercure de France, during the first half of December, announced Rousseau's Discourse as having just been printed. On this basis, it has customarily been concluded that the work appeared during the latter part of November, 1750. R. A. Leigh, however, has given convincing reasons in favor of the actual publication having been withheld until about January 8, 1751

(Leigh, *Corr.*, II, 135. Cf. pp. 136–40). Pissot, in a letter of the middle of the month, explains that he is just sending a copy to the Director of French Publications, M. de Malesherbes. He would hardly have waited for six weeks to fulfill such an evident obligation. Similarly, a letter by Rousseau of January 19 to the Academy of Dijon gives his long illness in explanation of the delay in publication and in supplying the Academy with the required copies.

III *Summary of Rousseau's Discourse*

The author begins with an apology to the learned Academy for taking the negative of the question. He writes: "It is not knowledge that I am attacking, I have said to myself, but virtue that I am defending in the presence of virtuous men." To see mankind dissipate by the light of reason the darkness of ignorance around him is a great spectacle, but, alas: men have not become better. Instead, a veil of false politeness has taken the place of sincerity, and a dangerous skepticism has been substituted for the ignorance which men have come to despise. The early Germans, praised by Tacitus, the first Persians, the Scythians, Sparta, primitive Rome, these were traditional examples of a wholesome simplicity and courage before degeneration set in. These offered the happy ignorance cherished by Socrates and by the elder Cato. What would the great Fabricius have thought if he could have returned to that simpler Rome which he had known so well? The political writers of ancient times talked only of morals and virtue; ours speak of nothing but commerce and money.

"Tell us, O famous Arouet," as Rousseau surprisingly invoked Voltaire under his original family name, "how many strong and manly beauties you have sacrificed to our false delicacy, and how much the spirit of elegance, so productive of petty things, has cost you the presence of those that are great." Even a dangerous inequality has raised its ugly head in our society, Rousseau notes in passing, thus forecasting his coming second Discourse, but it is a charge he does not here develop further.

We no longer ask whether a man is honest, Jean-Jacques continues, but whether he possesses talents, not whether a book is useful, but whether it is well written. True, a few great writers are capable of dealing with knowledge. Let them be committed to the study of the arts and sciences; let them be chosen to guide kings and rulers of peoples in sound government. Finally, Rousseau concludes with an eloquent tribute to virtue, that sublime knowledge appropriate to the spirits of the simple. Are not the principles of virtue engraved on all hearts? Does it not suffice to listen to the voice of conscience while the passions are silent? Here is true philosophy. Let us be content with it. Let us try, he adds, in an unacknowledged quotation of his favorite Montaigne, "let us try to make between those celebrated men of letters and ourselves that glorious distinction observed in former times between two great peoples: that one knew how to speak well, the other, how to do well."[2] Thus Rousseau, like Montaigne, awards the palm to ancient Sparta over its gifted rival, Athens.

Diderot enthusiastically reported to Rousseau the surprising reception of his Discourse. "It is praised to the skies," he said; "there has never been a success like it!" There were many who agreed with Jean-Jacques in his severe criticism of society. Others, more vocal, were shocked at his attack on the modern progress of which they were so proud. A host of refutations appeared in print.

One of these rebuttals came unexpectedly from Stanislas, ex-King of Poland, now ruler of the small province of Lorraine on the eastern border of France and father-in-law of King Louis XV himself. Rousseau felt much honored. At the same time, he published a reply, mingling with dignity frankness and respect. "Knowledge is good in itself," Rousseau admitted. "There are a few distinguished minds for whom it is suitable, but for the average man it is enough to study his duties," contenting himself thus with a life of simplicity and virtue. A people, once corrupted and launched on the downward path, has never been known to recover.

Stanislas, after reading Rousseau's reply, is said to have remarked without anger: "I've got what was coming to me; I'll not rub him the wrong way again."

Another refutation came from a Professor Gautier, otherwise unknown to us. He was a specialist in history and effectively laid bare Rousseau's grave weaknesses in that field. But Rousseau treated him with high-handed contempt. In a letter to his friend Grimm, Rousseau reiterated the contention of his Discourse, already in his opinion decisive, and concluded: "So I'll not reply to M. Gautier." In a postscript he added for good measure: "I still conclude that I have no need to reply to M. Gautier." Rousseau's adversary, by no means quelled, retorted with a second reply, even stronger than the first, but Jean-Jacques wisely remained silent.

Another refutation came, however, from Rousseau's old friend at Lyons, Charles Borde. "We have long since given up belief in the chimera of a Golden Age," wrote Borde. "How can we admire the grossness of the early Scythians and Persians?" Vice and corruption are found wherever there are men, but they are not due to knowledge. "There is only ignorance which is not good for anything." Borde praised the new project of the *Encyclopedia* which certainly aimed at the spread of knowledge. Mention of the *Encyclopedia* struck close to home since it was known that Diderot was its director. Rousseau himself indeed had consented to write the articles on music, though of this Borde may perhaps not have been as yet informed. And Borde attacked war. He did not laud war as an example of strength and courage, a position Jean-Jacques had taken in his Discourse when dealing with ancient Rome. Borde held up war as a surviving relic of barbarism, which ought at last to be abandoned.

In his reply Rousseau courteously paid his respects to his old friend and to the strength of his arguments. "Knowledge does indeed represent the height of genius and reason," agreed Rousseau. "If it were cultivated by men of genius and of ideal character, only good would result," but "evil men use it for much that is harmful while those who are good draw from it little advantage." Private property, which has developed with society, is harmful. "*Thine* and *mine* are frightful words." The citizen of Geneva agrees with Borde that wars of conquest are evil. He stands now clearly for wars of self-defense only. This distinction he had not made in his Discourse. It represents an important progress in his thinking and a progress due evidently to Borde. True knowledge is good, agreed Rousseau, "but I am speaking of the kind we have." Finally, "I have pointed out the evil and its causes. Let others, bolder, if not wiser, endeavor to find the remedy."

The *Mercure de France* in May of 1752 commented with respect: "M. Rousseau's character unfortunately gives weight to his criticism. He is a sincere man and is well informed."

But on September 14, 1751 (Leigh, II, p. 163, n. b), we find Voltaire replying contemptuously to the Duke d'Uzès, who had called his attention to the publication of Rousseau's Discourse: "I am hardly in a position, at the court of the King of Prussia, to read themes composed by school boys for prizes offered by the Academy of Dijon," the backward "school boy" being at the time thirty-nine years old! Naturally, Voltaire did read the Discourse, however, and, amidst more cursory thrusts, made one penetrating comment on Rousseau: "I saw here a man who started by hating the abuse of the arts and came in the end to hate the arts themselves."

Other refutations followed thick and fast. To some of them Rousseau continued to reply. The extraordinary stir aroused by his First Discourse kept him busy. The controversy had one constructive aspect. It obliged him to reflect and to clarify further his ideas. Gradually he formed what he called in the *Confessions* his "great program." He revealed himself to be a forceful debater and learned increasingly to write with originality and vigor.

What remains of Rousseau's Discourse today? Clearly we cannot accept his position in favor of primitive life. His argument, as he admitted later in the *Confessions*, is weak, "but with whatever talent one may be born," he added, "the art of writing is not to be learned all at once." What remains for us in the First Discourse is its emphasis on moral instead of mere material progress. In face of the great advances in speed and comfort of transportation, with the welter of new inventions developed by modern science, confronted by the marvels of rapid speech communication, we easily forget that these changes do not necessarily make life better at its core. Modern bombs and guns and tanks and planes only render war more terrible than in the days of the club, the arrow, or the flintlock of the past. We still have to struggle against economic and racial inequality, legal injustice, and all the problems of disunity. The eighteenth century ended in the fearful explosion of the French Revolution. We cannot know what the twentieth century may still hold in store. For ourselves, we must cherish the hope of being able to show the moral, as well as the material strength that preeminence in the modern world demands. This is still the vital challenge of Rousseau's *Discourse on the Arts and Sciences.*

IV   The Quarrel over French versus Italian Music

In the midst of the heated debate over the First Discourse, there came a strange interlude. This was the quarrel over French versus Italian music. Rousseau, after his years in Italy, was strongly in favor of the beauty of Italian language and the singing charm of Italian melody. In this opinion Grimm joined him, with more humor and less conviction. Diderot also was with them, true, but with no deep concern. An Italian light opera company called without derogatory meaning the "Buffoons," from "Opera Buffa" (comic opera), gave its popular plays in Paris beginning in the summer of 1752.

Meanwhile, following the successful controversy over the First Discourse, Rousseau astonished everyone by deciding to put his conduct in harmony with his attack on conventional society. He gave up white stockings and gold lace, adopted a plain round wig, abandoned wearing a sword and sold his watch, saying to himself "with unbelievable delight, thank Heaven, I'll not need to know the time of day anymore." Inapt to practice the complex manners of existing society, as he frankly confesses, "I decided to take on manners of my own, which would make me independent of them. . . . I affected to despise the politeness which I did not know how to practice." His friends were surprised to see him take seriously what they regarded only as a prize essay.

For some ten years Rousseau had been occupied off and on with a one-act comedy, *Narcisse, ou l'Amant de lui-même (Narcissus, or the Man in Love with Himself)*. Repeatedly, he had rewritten or revised the play to make it stage-worthy. Finally on December 18, 1752, it had the honor of being played by the Comédie-Française and seemed at last on its way to winning at least moderate favor. Jean-Jacques, however, strangely bored, as he confessed, at the first performance, made a rare virtue of frankness and astonished everyone across the street from the Comédie at the famous Café Procope by being the first to label it publicly a failure. The play was withdrawn after the second performance. The journalist Fréron commented wittily that Rousseau, in contrast to other authors, took pride in his ill success. This incident was a further element in his "reform" after the First Discourse. Early in 1753, however, he published an important *Preface to Narcissus* which, though having little to do with the comedy, further clarified his favorite ideas on the "natural goodness" of man and the corruption attributed to the arts and sciences.

Quite rapidly and easily now Rousseau wrote a brief musical piece called *Le Devin du village* (*The Village Soothsayer*). It may be described as French words set to Italian music. The play became at once popular, was given by command before the King and Court at Fontainebleau in October of 1752, was presented later at Court with Mme de Pompadour playing the role of Colin, and at the Paris Opera in March, 1753, for the general public. Rousseau attended by invitation the performance at Fontainebleau, sitting in a box in full view of the audience. He wore his newly adopted careless clothes, a beard, and uncombed wig. At first he was ill at ease, but, telling himself he was in his proper place in his usual costume, he talked himself into composure. The play was very successful and the audience most kind. The next day he was to be received by the King and given a pension. This prospect, however, with fear of his physical incontinence and embarrassment at not knowing what to say before the King, gave him a sleepless night. The next day he fled from Fontainebleau, abandoning any thought of a pension in spite of the outspoken objections of his friend Diderot. In fact, this dispute was the cause of their first quarrel.

The *Village Soothsayer* was a distinct monetary success also. Rousseau received one hundred louis from the King for the performance at Fontainebleau, fifty from Mme de Pompadour for the staging in which she took part at Court, fifty more from the Opera, some two thousand francs in all, plus five hundred francs from his publisher Pissot (Pléiade, I, p. 386, n.4). The franc in purchasing power may well have been more than the equivalent of today's dollar so that this brief musical interlude became Rousseau's chief support for several years. He comments that this piece which cost him no more than five or six weeks of work brought him almost as much money as his great educational treatise of *Emile* (1762) on which he spent twenty years of reflection and three years of work.

All the next day after the performance of the *Soothsayer* at Fontainebleau, King Louis went about singing its leading airs, singing, Rousseau's informant said, "in a voice more off-key than any other in his kingdom." The play was indeed a triumphant success and Jean-Jacques's thoughts inevitably went back to that time twenty years before at the home of M. de Treytorens near Lausanne when he had been so humiliated by the caterwauling of the orchestra which he had rashly tried to conduct without knowing how. What a change!

Toward the end of 1753 Rousseau published an essay entitled "Letter on French Music." Nothing more legitimate than to make known his strong preference for the music of Italy. Unfortunately, instead of adopting a gracious and persuasive tone, he chose to write in a combative and abusive style which could only anger, not convince his opponents. French singing, he charges, is "a continual barking," its harmony is "brutish," without expression. The female star in her leading aria gives way to a loud "bawling." The whole is a complete "cacophony." From all this, he concludes "that the French have no music and cannot have any or, if they ever do have a music of their own, it will be so much the worse for them."

As if this were not enough, Rousseau also published in this same autumn of 1753 a supposedly half-facetious *Letter of a Symphony Player of the Royal Academy of Music to his Orchestra Comrades.* Under this pretense of writing from within the Opera's own orchestra, he openly calls in question their professional competence. The violinists are mere "scrapers of catgut." Their music "grates" on the audience's ears. To cap the climax, the first violin or concert master, who sets the tone for the other players, is "deaf." The result of their labors is a veritable "chivaree," the same word he had used of his own unfortunate efforts twenty years before.

Not unnaturally, the orchestra resented these repeated insults. In revenge, Rousseau was refused the free Opera pass to which he was entitled as a composer. In addition, he was hanged in effigy, was attacked in the streets, was beaten and kicked, as the Marquis d'Argenson recorded in his memoirs (Leigh, II, p. 324). His life even was reported in danger, and he moved about Paris under guard of a friendly officer of musketeers named Ancelet. The King too had changed his favorable attitude, now felt that Rousseau should be imprisoned as one of those free-thinking philosophers, ready to stir up an insurrection. There was actually talk of issuing a *lettre de cachet* to exile him from the kingdom; but the young Marquis de Voyer, a strong partisan of Italian music, persuaded his father, Comte d'Argenson, chief of police, that this would be carrying the noisy dispute to a ridiculous extreme (Leigh, II, p. 237, n). Over sixty brochures are said to have been issued in connection with this quarrel over music.[3] The uproar tended at any rate to take people's minds off the weightier controversy between the King and the judicial Parlement and may even have forestalled a tendency toward revolution already thought to be in the air (I, 384).

V *Rousseau's Second Discourse (1755)*

In this same November of 1753 the Dijon Academy again came to the fore. It offered a new subject of competition. The Academy now invited a prize discourse of three quarters of an hour reading time on the question: "What is the Origin of Inequality among Men and Whether it is Authorized by Natural Law?" Here was another topic just made for Rousseau, perhaps indeed proposed with him in mind. He had already, we recall, touched upon inequality in a passing sentence of his First Discourse. Now he was quite ready to return to it in more detail.

To reflect on this great question, Rousseau, with Thérèse, their hostess at the place where they were living, and another woman of their acquaintance, went for seven or eight days to Saint-Germain-en-Laye a few miles down the Seine from Paris. Saint-Germain, some three hundred feet above the river, offered an invigorating and healthful atmosphere. While the three women took care of the meals, Rousseau, in perfect freedom, wandered in the great forest with its centuries-old oak trees, imagining himself a man of nature, living the primeval life of which he had dreamed. His mind filled with the popular voyage literature of the time, Jean-Jacques, unlike the war-like Hurons or Iroquois, easily pictured himself similar to the indolent natives of the Caribbean, getting his meals without labor in a kindly and friendly climate. The tropical fruits and luxuriant vegetation, which Saint-Germain could not furnish, Rousseau easily recreated in imagination from memories of the Royal Zoological Garden, presided over now in Paris by the great naturalist Buffon.

So the Second Discourse, the *Discourse on Inequality*, gradually came into being. Diderot, too, felt a hatred of social inequality, though not in quite the same intense fashion as Rousseau. Diderot also cherished at times the fantasy of an exotic life, but more after the mood or spirit of "the mystic isles of the South Seas" with beautiful amorous maidens rather than the idle Caribs of Jean-Jacques's creation. Diderot, besides, was interested in science, the slowly expanding knowledge depicted in his contemporary book, *Thoughts on the Interpretation of Nature* (1754). So he had much to pass along to Rousseau when the latter consulted him, and he agreed with him fully on the dangers of tyranny in government. Hence we can well understand that, in the author's words, his *Discourse on Inequality* "was more to the taste of Diderot" than any of his other works, up to that time at least, and the one "for which his suggestions were the most useful." Later, after their quarrel, Rousseau was to interpret his earlier comment unfavorably, feeling that Diderot was responsible for making his *Discourse* more bitter and cynical than it might otherwise have been. We need not take this biased opinion too seriously.

There are, says Rousseau near the beginning of his *Discourse*, two kinds of inequality. There is a natural inequality, dependent upon age, strength of body, mind, or health, and this inequality must be accepted as largely unalterable. There is also another kind of inequality, which may be labeled moral or political inequality. This inequality is artificial. It is the creation of society. This it is which creates existing differences in wealth, rank, privilege, or the right to rule or be obeyed. This is the inequality which Rousseau is now set to discuss and attack.

"Let us begin," writes Jean-Jacques, "by putting aside all the facts, for they have no bearing on the question." This statement, as one may well imagine, has caused much spilling of ink by opponents of Rousseau. Its meaning, however, is quite different from what might be supposed if it is taken in isolation out of context. All it means is that Rousseau does not intend to treat the question from what might be called the orthodox "Biblical facts" of the first chapters of *Genesis*. If indeed he had done that, no discussion would have been possible. Instead, he presents the slow development of humanity over many unknown ages of time, but he can do so, he assures the reader, only on a basis of conjecture. Thus, like Descartes in the seventeenth century or like Buffon just a few years before him, Rousseau sought to avoid the dangerous charge of heresy.

Proceeding with his argument, Rousseau does not, like Aristotle, ask whether man at first was equipped with "hooked claws, was hairy like a bear and walked on four feet." Instead, he starts with man constituted as he is today so far as his physical organism is concerned. Unlike the English philosopher Hobbes, Rousseau believes man in the state of nature was at peace with his fellows rather than at war. He also enjoyed more freedom from illness than in civilized society. In fact, "I will almost dare to assert," says Rousseau, "that the state of reflection is a state contrary to nature, and that the man who meditates is an animal in a state of depravity or decline." Too often the last half of this statement has been quoted out of context with disastrous results for Rousseau. All it means, however, is that study and reflection are harmful to man's health if carried to an extreme without the proper balance of physical activity or exercise. As often happens, Jean-Jacques expressed his thought in such unusual fashion and with such vigor that his perfectly natural meaning can easily be distorted. Already in his *Preface* to the play *Narcissus,* he had said more clearly: "Study wears out man's physical machine, . . . and that alone shows clearly that it is not made for us."

It must have taken long centuries for man to develop even the art of agriculture. And what of language? Rousseau was influenced by his friend and contemporary philosopher Condillac, but in the end found himself unable to determine how language could have been developed "by purely human means." Was it society which caused language to take form or did languages lead to the creation of society?

Contrary to most other thinkers, Rousseau, without long experience of family life himself, believes that primitive man was an isolated being wandering largely alone in the state of nature, but not unhappy. At first neither bad nor good, he gradually developed pity for any misfortunes or illnesses he saw in his fellow man and so came to a simple moral code. "Do good to yourself with the least possible harm to others" appeared to Rousseau a more practical and attainable rule of good conduct than the high-principled Golden Rule. In primitive life, love was simple, free of the complex problems created by society. With society, inequality, hardly perceptible among early men, came into being and increased with the development of human institutions. Here the First Part of the Second Discourse ends.

At the beginning of the Second Part, Rousseau gives expression to a vigorous attack on private property. "The first man," he says, "who inclosed a piece of ground and took it into his head to say: *This is mine,* and found people simple enough to believe him, was the true founder of civil society. How many crimes, wars, murders, miseries, and horrors would have been spared the human race by him who, pulling up the stakes or filling in the boundary ditch, would have said to his fellows: 'Take good care not to listen to this imposter; you are lost if you forget that the fruits belong to everybody and the land to no one.'"

Voltaire, when he read these revolutionary words, scribbled in anger on the margin of his copy: "What, he who planted, sowed, and staked in, has no right to the fruits of his labor! What! this unjust man, this thief, would have been considered the benefactor of the human race! That's the philosophy of a beggar who would like to see the rich robbed by the poor!" Obviously, the owner of Les Délices on the borders of Geneva, the future lord of Ferney and Count of Tournay, the appointed Gentleman of the King's Bedchamber and member of the French Academy, had no use for Rousseau's unsettling doctrine. In witty, if more polite language, he would express his thought to Rousseau himself shortly in a famous letter of acknowledgment which we shall refer to later.

If this passage startled and shocked Voltaire, it no doubt aroused the anger of the members of the Dijon Academy no less. At any rate, promptly rejecting the Discourse as "too long and of a bad tradition," they proceeded with pleasure to give the prize to the Abbé Talbert, who had competed unsuccessfully in 1750, but now at last came into his own with an orthodox justification of the inequality which Rousseau so outspokenly condemned.

In his Second Discourse, Rousseau, under the influence no doubt of his old friend Borde and his refutation of the First Discourse, encouraged also by Diderot, attacked vigorously wars of aggression, which he had not singled out when he had praised the military virtues of the ancient Romans five years before. With the idea of a contract implicit between people and rulers, he laid the foundation for outlawing the long-existing theory of the "divine right of kings" which Louis XV still asserted with old-time assurance. To the recalcitrant judicial Parlement, the King indeed declared firmly: "I know all the rights of authority which I derive from God. It befits none of my subjects to limit or decide how far they extend." Yet less than fifty years would see these so-called "rights" overthrown.

Finally, in his last paragraph, Rousseau emphasized once again his dependence on conjecture, free from the influence of the Biblical text of Genesis. "I have tried," he says, "to show the origin and progress of inequality, the establishment of the abuses due to political society, insofar as these can be deduced from the nature of man through the sole light of reason and independent of the sacred dogmas which give to sovereign authority the sanction of divine right." So much for the censor, the "sacred dogmas," and the "divine right of kings." Inequality, almost non-existent in the state of nature, gradually increases with the development of society and is contrary to any sense of justice whenever it is out of proportion with those purely natural inequalities of health, strength, and ability which Rousseau had named at the beginning of his Discourse. Once more, as at the end of his Discourse on the Arts and Sciences, he closed with a vigorous, but unnamed quotation from Montaigne. "It is manifestly contrary to the law of nature," he wrote, "in whatever way one defines it, that an infant should give orders to his elders, an imbecile should rule over a man of sense, and a handful of people should be gorged with superfluities while the starving multitude lacks what is necessary."[4]

Rousseau's Second Discourse drew some refutations, but not of the same number or interest as those which had greeted the First. Even Voltaire, in his famous letter of acknowledgment, refrained from discussing the central question of inequality. Instead, he turned back toward the earlier *Discourse on the Arts and Sciences*, but here he did not dwell on Rousseau's theme. He noted rather the jealousies and unjust attacks which too often beset the writer of genius. Voltaire begins his letter under date of August 30, 1755: "I have received, Sir, your new book against the human race. I thank you for it."

In the published version, Voltaire then made a few slight retouches to heighten the effect—retouches which were not in the original copy received by Rousseau. "You will give men pleasure by telling them well-deserved truths," the master of Les Délices continues, "but you will not correct them. It is impossible to depict in stronger colors the shortcomings of human society from which our ignorance and our weakness promise us such consolation. Never has anyone shown such wit to reduce us to animal stupidity. One feels like walking on all fours after reading your work. However, as it is now more than sixty years since I have lost this habit, I feel unfortunately that it is impossible for me to resume it, and I leave this natural gait to those more worthy of it than you or I. Neither can I take ship to seek out the savages of Canada, first because the maladies with which I am afflicted keep me near the greatest physician in Europe and I should not find the same help among the Missouris; secondly, because war has been carried into those countries and the example of our nations has rendered the savages almost as bad as ourselves. I limit myself to being a peaceful savage in the solitude which I have chosen near your country where you ought to be."

"M. Chappuis [who had delivered Rousseau's Discourse to Voltaire] tells me that your health is very bad. You must come and regain it in your native air, enjoy our liberty, drink with me the milk of our cows, and graze on our herbs" (Leigh, III, 156–58).

It was a clever letter, one never to be forgotten in its skillful mingling of satire with the external forms of politeness. Rousseau answered it promptly and by no means unworthily on September 7.

"It is for me to thank you, Sir, on all counts," he wrote. "In offering you my gloomy reflections, I had no thought of making a present worthy of you, but only of fulfilling a duty and of rendering you a homage which all of us owe you as our chief. . . . Do not try to fall back to walking on all fours. Nobody in the world would be less successful at it than you. You teach us too well to walk erect on our two feet and should not cease to stand on your own." There follow two pages of serious argument along Rousseau's own lines, after which he closes with a reference to Voltaire's invitation to return to Geneva.

"I am grateful for your invitation, and if this winter leaves me well enough in the spring to go and live in my native country, I shall take advantage of your kindness. But I should rather drink the water from your fountain than the milk from your cows, and as to the herbs in your garden, I very much fear finding only the lotus, which is not good feed for animals, and the moly, which prevents men from becoming like them" (Leigh, III, 164–68).

So Jean-Jacques closed with a reference to Homer's tempting food of the lotus, which it was almost impossible for men to abandon eating, and the moly, which protected Ulysses from the dangerous enchantments of Circe. Such, Rousseau politely suggests, would be the result of a stay under the captivating charm of Voltaire's rare genius and flashing wit.

This exchange of letters was shortly published by the patriarch of Les Délices with the ready permission of Rousseau. The latter was no doubt proud of having successfully crossed swords with his famous antagonist. Thus relations between the two writers continued for the time being friendly in spite of their profound intellectual differences.

As for Rousseau's *Discourse on Inequality*, we can hardly measure with exactness its influence in the eighteenth century.

It seems fair to conclude, however, that it must have given a strong further push to the movement in favor of equality which was already in the air. Along with *liberté* and *fraternité*, we cannot forget that the French Revolution was to give similar place to *égalité*, and the work of Rousseau was prominent in the thought of Robespierre and other revolutionary leaders.

VI *Rousseau's Article on* Political Economy *(1755)*

Rousseau's article on *Political Economy* appeared in Volume V of the *Encyclopedia*, which was distributed to subscribers in November, 1755 (III, pp. lxxii and 1864). Since it took a good ten months for a volume of the *Encyclopedia* to go through its various stages of printing and proof reading, we can infer that the manuscript must have been completed by the end of 1754 or earlier. It was thus practically contemporary with the text of the *Discourse on Inequality* which had been put into the hands of the Amsterdam printer Rey in October, 1754. Rousseau had written his article with particular pleasure. To his friend, the young Genevan pastor, Jacob Vernes, he said in a letter of March 28, 1756, "You like my article on *Economics*. I can well understand that. It was my heart that dictated it and yours that read it" (Leigh, III, p. 308).

There is a great difference, comments Rousseau in his article, in spite of what some authors claim, between a family ruled over by a father and a political body governed by its head. The author first wrote boldly: "In an hereditary *crown*, we often find an infant in command of men." Before publication, someone, presumably the editor Diderot, conscious of the censor, changed the dangerous word "crown" to the less incriminating "magistracy." Similarly, Rousseau posed this disquieting question: "I do not know whether human wisdom has ever made a good king." Here once again, his challenging passage was altered to read: "But from the beginning of the world, human wisdom has made very few good magistrates."[5] Both of these passages, in their original form, seem, with their references to "an infant" or "an imbecile" ruling over men of maturity or good sense, to spring from persistent memories of the vigorous quotation from

Montaigne with which Rousseau had concluded his *Discourse on Inequality.*

In this article, Rousseau lays stress on the important principle of the General Will, later to play such a significant part in his *Social Contract* (1762). This General Will is synonymous with the General Welfare of the people at large. How shall we determine what this General Will is? We can hardly in a big country assemble all the citizens for discussion or vote. But Rousseau believes that the ruler, if he is just, will be able readily to determine for himself where the welfare of the people at large lies. It is to be noted that in this same fifth volume of the *Encyclopedia* an article by Diderot entitled *Droit naturel* (*Natural Right*) also used this same term General Will, the result perhaps of many intimate discussions of the two friends together. Although there are in Diderot's evidently previously-written article some ideas which Rousseau refutes, he nevertheless makes a direct cross-reference to it in one of his early pages.

"It is certain that nations in the long run become what their government causes them to be" (III, 251). This idea had become a fundamental principle of Rousseau's thought ever since his experience as Secretary to the French Ambassador at Venice. There he had observed the effect on its people of the Venetian government with the contrasting results observed in Geneva and France. References to this dominating effect of government are repeated in the "Preface to Narcissus" (II, 969), later in the *Confessions* (I, 404–405), and now here in the article on *Political Economy* (III, 251).

How shall we cause the General Will to be realized, asks Rousseau? We must implant virtue as an effective force in the minds of the people. The idea is evidently a reminiscence of Montesquieu's *Spirit of Laws* (1748) with his emphasis on virtue as the necessary motive force of a democratic government. But laws should not be multiplied to excess. This action will lead only to their being viewed with contempt. Citizens will become good when they have been taught to love their country. Only in governments where freedom is preserved, do we find a true value put upon the individual citizen. Such was above all the case with ancient Rome. Public education must be established to produce this civic spirit.

After Rousseau's violent denunciation of private property in his *Discourse on Inequality*, we observe with some surprise that the protection of property is declared in his article to be the essential basis of civil society. But in his previous work, the author had been dealing with a theoretical state of nature. Here, as later in the *Social Contract* and in *Emile*, he is strictly practical. He has evidently come to see that, on freedom to work, to acquire property, and to retain it within reason, depends the preservation of life itself.

As one might expect, Rousseau declares that "to describe the economic system of a good government," he has "often turned his eyes back" to his native country of Geneva as an example of what he would like to see passed along to all other nations.

Taxes should be graduated according to income, calculated to decrease the tendency toward "the continual augmentation of inequality of wealth." Taxes on land used for agriculture should not be excessive. One should follow in this respect the examples of Holland and England, and, above all, of China where the cutlivation of the land, believes Rousseau, is at its best. Articles of luxury, especially, should be taxed in order to preserve a proper distinction, dear to the eighteenth century, between "the necessary and the superfluous."

All in all, while somewhat rambling, Rousseau, in his article, insists boldly on the liberty of peoples, as against the authority of their kings or rulers, lays down the principle of the General Will, which is passed on later to his *Social Contract* (1762), encourages a rural agriculture over manufacturing in cities, and insists on taxes graduated to combat luxury and inequality of wealth.

VII   *The Earthquake at Lisbon (1755)*

On November 1, 1755, there was a terrible earthquake in Lisbon, followed by flooding from waves in the harbor. After that came disastrous fires springing from the numerous candles in the churches celebrating All Saints' Day and from the overturning of stoves used for cooking or heating. The fires indeed were not extinguished for nearly a week after the earthquake and were responsible for much material damage.[6] Loss of life, at first greatly exaggerated in terms of 100,000 people, in the end still remained high at 10,000 to 15,000 with many more who were seriously injured. It was a terrible calamity which lingered in the minds of all Europe and posed the soul-shaking question of how, if God is good, such a great human tragedy could be permitted to occur.

In the churches of Switzerland, France, Germany, and England, as well as in Portugal itself, preachers struggled with this question in their sermons. Few took their stand on natural causes alone in connection with earthquakes. Indeed, few could yet agree on what these causes were. The question was further complicated by a widespread belief in the philosophy of optimism as exemplified by the German Leibniz or by the even better known Alexander Pope in his poem, the "Essay on Man" (1733–1734).

This philosophy of optimism should not be understood in the ordinary sense of the word as meaning that everything is perfect. Rather the thought was that God in his wisdom must have made everything for the best, that this world, though it contains evil, must be the "best of all possible worlds" conceivable. Thus Pope in the "Essay on Man":

> All Nature is but Art, unknown to thee;
> All Chance, Direction, which thou canst not see;
> All Discord, Harmony not understood;
> All partial Evil, universal Good:
> And spite of Pride, in erring Reason's spite,
> One truth is clear, WHATEVER IS, IS RIGHT.

Voltaire had known Pope in England. He was also very familiar with his poem, which indeed he had imitated freely in his own *Discours sur l'homme* of 1738–1739 with many revisions in the years following. Thus, though in his earlier lifetime, he had been inclined to look upon the philosophy of optimism with some degree of favor, particularly as it was adopted by his mistress, Mme du Châtelet, he could not now with equanimity see it applied to the Lisbon earthquake. So, shortly after the slow-traveling news reached him on November 23–24 (two weeks from Lisbon to Paris and another week from Paris to Geneva), he began composing his own "sermon" in the shape of his famous *Poem on the Disaster of Lisbon* (1756). In this poem of two hundred and thirty-four lines, he expresses his deep shock at the earthquake and his sympathy with suffering humanity at Lisbon. His grief and puzzlement are only slightly mitigated at the end by some not very convincing lines on Hope, added late in the composition of the poem in order to satisfy the censor and appease, if appeasement were possible, Pastor Elie Bertrand, Dr. Theodore Tronchin, and other friends or acquaintances in Switzerland.

On the ninth of April, 1756, Rousseau, Thérèse, and the aged Mme Levasseur had been transported by carriage to a place north of Paris in the nearby countryside, the Hermitage, offered him by his wealthy friend, Mme d'Epinay. Rousseau was delighted to be rid of the noise and congestion of the big city, enchanted with the quiet and beauty of the country. Only then, he wrote later to Malesherbes, Director of Publication, did he "begin to live." It was rather cold still in this early April and patches of snow lingered in shady spots, but grass, trees, and bushes were showing a fresh green, buds were opening, while here and there violets and gay primroses pushed up toward the warm sun. Early on this first morning Rousseau listened with rare pleasure as the nightingale sang. Tramping alone through the woods, Rousseau began thinking of his various literary projects and composing passages in his mind, or making brief notes, as he liked to do.

Early in July Rousseau received, through the intermediary of a friend Duclos, two poems by Voltaire published together, one the *Poem on the Disaster of Lisbon* and another written three or four years earlier, the *Poem on Natural Law*, or as it was at first too boldly called, *Poem on Natural Religion*. On June 4, 1756, Voltaire wrote to his friend and factotum in Paris, Thieriot, sending him copies of the new edition of his "sermons," as he facetiously labeled his two poems, and asking him to distribute them to Diderot, d'Alembert, and Rousseau. Thieriot replied on June 21: "Within a few days I'll pass along to our good friends, Diderot and d'Alembert, their copies along with that to Diogenes Rousseau." Thus Thieriot, aware of Rousseau's withdrawal to the country and his drift away from the *philosophes*, placed Jean-Jacques in a special category of isolation in a way that Voltaire at this time had not done. The master of Les Délices, in fact, had put all three men on the same plane, adding a precautionary sentence: "They will understand me well enough; they will see that I could not express myself differently, and they will be edified by a few footnotes; they will not denounce these *sermons*." Thus Voltaire referred to the fact that, to appease the censor and his Swiss friends, he had felt obliged to appear more orthodox than he really was. Uninformed of Rousseau's newly developed religious views, Voltaire feared that Jean-Jacques, as well as Diderot and d'Alembert, might think their old leader, not too radical, but too prudent in his religious philosophy. They will all three read between the lines, he hopes. They will understand that he has said as much as he dared, that he implies more than he has said.

On July 6, Thieriot wrote again to Voltaire saying that he had given "the three copies of your excellent sermons to the three learned doctors Diderot, d'Alembert, and Rousseau." Since Rousseau, however, was now out in the country, Thieriot had passed his copy to a friend named Duclos who was going out to visit Jean-Jacques and asked as a favor to be allowed to take the poems to him. So it was that by this date of Sunday, July 6, or shortly after, Rousseau had received Voltaire's two poems and was in a position to reflect on their content. He had some six weeks to prepare a long letter in reply which he finally sent to Voltaire under date of August 18, 1756.

VIII   *Rousseau's Letter to Voltaire on Providence*

Rousseau begins his letter rather surprisingly: "Your two most recent poems, Sir, have reached me in my solitary retreat, and although my friends know the love that I have for your writings, I do not know where they could have come from except from yourself." Unless either Thieriot or Duclos had singularly failed in their mission to deliver Voltaire's message to

Rousseau, there is no way that Jean-Jacques could not have known the source of the two poems. The only explanation of his opening sentence seems to be one of prudence. Perhaps he thought simply that Voltaire might find it advisable to disavow them if their reception became too hot. As a matter of fact, three years later, the *Poem on Natural Law*, seemingly the less offensive of the two poems, was condemned by the French censor.

For Rousseau, at any rate, the *Poem on Natural Law* pleased him immensely. It accorded well with his own ideas. "All my objections, therefore, are directed against your *Poem on the Disaster at Lisbon*," he writes. "You reproach Pope and Leibniz with adding to our ills by insisting that all is for the best and you multiply the toll of our sufferings to such an extent that you increase our consciousness of them. Instead of the consolation for which I hoped, you merely increase my affliction. One would think that you are afraid I would not see how unfortunate I am. You believe, it seems, that you will bring me great comfort by proving to me that everything is evil."

But just the contrary is what happens. Rousseau finds comfort in optimism. "The poem by Pope lessens my sufferings and teaches me patience. Your poem increases my pain, stimulates me to protest, and, taking from me everything except an enfeebled hope, reduces me to despair."

> You do not, Sir, wish your work to be considered a poem against Providence, and I shall take good care not to give it such a name, although you qualified as a book against the human race a work in which I pleaded the cause of the human race against itself. . . . In depicting the troubles of humanity, my aim was excusable and even praiseworthy, I believe, for I showed men how they created their misfortunes themselves, and consequently how they could avoid them.

Thus Rousseau took advantage of the opening granted him by Voltaire to reveal that he still resented the thrust against the *Discourse on Inequality* made in the latter's witty letter of a year ago even though Jean-Jacques had refrained from taking it up at the time.

In his next paragraph, Rousseau sees the cause of moral evil in man's freedom of the will, and physical evil also to a great extent as the work of man himself. He urges Voltaire:

Without quitting your subject of Lisbon, agree that it was not nature that put twenty thousand six-story houses there and that, if the inhabitants of this great city had been scattered more evenly or lodged in more lightly constructed buildings, the damage would have been much less and perhaps even nil. . . . How many unfortunates have perished in this disaster in order to save, some their clothes, some their papers, others their money? Do we not know that the person of each man has become the least part of him and that it is not worth while to save himself if he loses all the rest?

All this seems rather heartless on the part of Rousseau and, in his desire to prove his point, Jean-Jacques shows himself quite lacking in sympathy for the unfortunate victims of Lisbon. This attitude is in sharp contrast to the deep feeling of Voltaire evident in his poem.

Men of letters, most sedentary in occupation, unhealthy, too reflective, may be discontented with life and the universe, Rousseau continues, but he doubts that such is the case with "a good bourgeois living a life obscure and tranquil," an artisan or a peasant, not of France, perhaps, "but of the country where you [Voltaire] now are," that is Switzerland. They would be quite content, Jean-Jacques feels, to live their life over, even if it may be, "in a kind of perpetual vegetation."

"The true principles of Optimism cannot be shown by the properties of matter or by the mechanism of the universe, but only by induction from the perfection of God who presides over all. Consequently, we do not prove the existence of God by the system of Pope, but the system of Pope by the existence of God.

"The question of Providence is connected with that of the immortality of the soul in which I [Rousseau] have the good fortune to believe without being ignorant of the fact that our reason may have doubts concerning it." On the other hand, neither he nor Voltaire, says Rousseau, nor any "man thinking rightly of God," can believe in the eternal punishment of mankind.

Rousseau, like Voltaire, is strongly for tolerance, believing that man's religious beliefs should not be coerced, but left in perfect liberty. Then, strangely, he comes out for a kind of "civil religion" to establish a moral code and insure respect and observance of the laws, "a catechism of the citizen," which Voltaire, he suggests, might wish to draw up as the last and greatest of all his works.

In closing, Rousseau observes a remarkable contrast between Voltaire and himself. Voltaire is surfeited with glory, disabused of all vain grandeur, living freely in the midst of abundance, sure of literary immortality, philosophizing peacefully over the nature of the soul, and if body or heart suffers, "you, Voltaire, have the great Tronchin as your doctor and your friend. Yet you find only evil in the world, while I, Rousseau, obscure, poor, solitary, tormented with an incurable illness, meditate with pleasure in my retreat, and find that all is for the best. Whence come these apparent contradictions? You have yourself explained it. You enjoy, but I hope, and hope embellishes everything."

This long letter was entrusted to Dr. Tronchin to deliver if he should think it wise. Tronchin did deliver it, though not encouraging Rousseau to believe it would change Voltaire's opinions. Voltaire replied briefly and courteously, but alleged his illness and that of his niece, Mme de Fontaine, as preventing him from debating with Rousseau at this time. He even half-apologized for his "mauvaises plaisanteries" directed a year ago at the *Discours sur l'inégalité*. Rousseau was at first delighted with the letter. He had not at any rate angered Voltaire, even though he was of course disappointed at not having persuaded the great man to debate with him. In fact, on September 20, 1756, he wrote to Mme d'Epinay: "I received yesterday a kind letter from Voltaire" (Leigh, IV, p. 112). Later, however, he asserted that Voltaire's real reply was his novel *Candide* (1759), "which," he insisted, "I have not read" (I, 430 and n. 1). As a matter of fact, though Voltaire did no doubt have Rousseau incidentally in mind while writing *Candide*, Jean-Jacques was quite wrong in thinking he occupied the center of the stage.

CHAPTER 3

In Full Career (1758–1762)

I *Rousseau's Letter to d'Alembert on the Theater (1758)*

AROUND the middle of August, 1756, d'Alembert visited Voltaire at Les Délices, spending a little over two weeks there or in nearby Geneva (Leigh, IV, 103, note c). D'Alembert's chief purpose was to gather material for an article on this unique Swiss city for the *Encyclopedia.*

Rousseau first heard of the article on Geneva from Diderot during the latter's final visit to the Hermitage on December 5. 1757 (Courtois, p. 97). Jean-Jacques comments in his *Confessions*: "He [Diderot] had told me that this article, agreed upon by Genevans of high rank, was aimed at the establishment of a theater in Geneva" (I, 494). Since Diderot seemed to approve and to have no doubt of the plan's success, Rousseau, having besides other much more personal grievances to discuss with his friend, made no rejoinder in regard to the theater, but waited impatiently for Volume VII of the *Encyclopedia,* which he received about December 20, 1757, soon after his sudden removal from the Hermitage to Mont-Louis at Montmorency (Courtois, p. 97). Rousseau thought d'Alembert's article "done with a good deal of skill and worthy of the pen from which it came" (I, 495). He decided nevertheless to reply, but in his own good time and without telling anyone in advance. He continues in the *Confessions*: "During a rather severe winter, in the month of February, ... I went every day for two hours in the morning and the same in the afternoon to an open Dungeon ... at the end of the garden where my dwelling was located. ... It was here in this frigid place, not sheltered from the wind and snow and without other fire than what was in my heart that, in the space of three weeks, I composed my *Letter to d'Alembert on the Theater*" (I, 495).

First Rousseau took up the charge of Socinianism or belief in the Unity of the Trinity of Father, Son, and Holy Ghost, lodged against some of the Protestant pastors by d'Alembert in the latter part of his article. Rousseau himself does not enter into the merits of this heresy, which he says do not interest him, but merely questions d'Alembert's right to reveal embarrassingly to the public what must have been confided to him in private conversation.

D'Alembert's article on *Geneva* is eight folio columns long. The part on the establishment of a theater in Geneva runs to nearly one folio column. Jean-Jacques wisely reprints this in a couple of pages of his *Preface* so that the reader can have it before him without the burden of seeking out the big, heavy volume of the *Encyclopedia* itself. Next the author proceeds to his counter argument against d'Alembert. The old contention that the theater is morally beneficial because it "purges the passions" is not true. Rather, the theater "purges the passions that we do not have and fosters those we have." An author who goes against the public's taste may write a very fine play, but it will be one that nobody will go to see. We tend to excuse the incest of Racine's Phèdre because of the intensity of her love. So with other French tragedies. Although Rousseau mentions several of Corneille's plays, he does not discuss them in detail, admitting that he has seen few of them on the stage, much as Corneille's strong-willed heroes might have been expected to appeal to him. But Rousseau, in this respect, like Voltaire, was very much of his own eighteenth century, strongly preferring the passion-tossed heroines of Racine.

Turning now to comedy, Rousseau emphasizes the necessity of drawing laughter from the standees crowded together in the parterre on the ground floor immediately in front of the stage. The phrase: "Il fallait faire rire le parterre" (We must make the people in the parterre laugh) is several times effectively repeated. In comedy, laughter is a prime necessity of success. Laughter excuses all.

Taking his example from the best of Molière's many excellent plays, Rousseau turns to the *Misanthrope*. Jean-Jacques willingly identifies himself with the frankness of Alceste while heaping scorn on the cautious tact of Philinte. What we need in society,

believes Rousseau, is more bold and even dangerous sincerity
rather than less. Other comedies of Molière can be still more
criticized from the moral point of view, but this does not mean
that Rousseau personally dislikes his plays. On the contrary,
he explains that he is enthusiastic about them and takes every
opportunity to see them on the stage in Paris. This very serious
Rousseau prizes the healing power of laughter. So he welcomes
too the ready comedy which the Italians have brought to the
French capital.

Rousseau recalls that a few years ago—it was on November 15,
1752 (Courtois, p. 68)—he and d'Alembert went together to a
performance of Racine's tragedy of *Bérénice* at the Comédie-
Française. As the play opens, says Rousseau, the spectator is
in a mood to look with contempt upon the Emperor Titus who
will even think of putting love before his duty as ruler of
Rome. At the end of the play, on the contrary, the reverse is
true. The spectator wonders why the great man does not retire
to private life happy in his requited love for the beautiful
Bérénice. In any case, concludes Rousseau, here is a clear case
where the theater stirs our emotions, but does not teach one
his duty. It is not fitted to increase the patriotic devotion of the
people of Geneva to their city-state.

In his *Encyclopedia* article d'Alembert had admitted that the
morals of actors, men and women, have been justly criticized.
He proposes as a remedy strict governmental regulation by the
police. Entirely ineffective, replied Rousseau. In such matters,
it is public opinion that decides, not law alone. Look at duels.
They have been forbidden since the preceding century, but
they still continue and will continue as long as honor demands
that a man must publicly resist an insult or incur a reputation
for cowardice.

Having shown the moral limitations both of plays and of
actors, Rousseau turns to a strong economic argument. Geneva,
admittedly, has at this time under 24,000 inhabitants; Paris has
over 600,000. Moreover, Paris is the capital of France, the
center of French literature and culture. Yet, in over ten years
of frequenting the theater regularly, Jean-Jacques has noted
difficulty on the part of the Comédie-Française, except on gala
occasions, in sustaining an average attendance of three hundred

spectators. With the competition of the Opera, the Italians, and, during part of the year, the popular Theater of the Fair, the total number of people attending these four spectacles on any one day would not exceed twelve hundred on the average, and from this figure must be deducted those authors and others who have the privilege of entering gratis. This attendance at Paris, Rousseau estimates, is the equivalent, in proportion to the population, of forty-eight persons as an average daily audience at Geneva. Can such a small number of people sustain a theater financially? The answer is obvious, and Rousseau's contention seems to have been supported even in modern times. With a greatly increased population, Geneva still has only a traveling company for a few months of the year and not a twelve-month permanent theater.

A good substitute, suggests Rousseau, in a long digression, is offered by the *cercles* or clubs. These keep men and women separate. This situation is better than their constant mingling socially in the salons, which, Jean-Jacques characteristically believes, tends to make men effeminate.

Big *fêtes* or festivals are also desirable in a republic like Geneva, says Rousseau. They help to develop national pride and patriotism. Moreover, they are held outdoors in a beautiful countryside and do not coop people up within a tightly enclosed building. Nor do they, like the theater, encourage constant expense for fine clothes as well as admission tickets. They do not regularly entice people away from their work which makes Geneva at present so prosperous.

Rousseau at first was very hesitant about the effectiveness of his *Letter to d'Alembert*, but it drew many replies, hostile or complimentary, and became one of the author's favorite works.

Voltaire, in spite of the repeated and sincere compliments Rousseau paid to his ability as a dramatist, was indignant. "What's this about Jean-Jacques's writing against the theater?" he exclaimed. "Has he become one of the Church Fathers?"

Diderot, favorable though he may have seemed at first to d'Alembert's article, found in Rousseau's opposing work an added obstacle to the success of his own dramatic efforts, *Le Fils naturel* (*The Natural Son*, 1757) and *Le Père de famille* (*The Father of the Family*, 1758). Indeed, Diderot came finally to regret the unnecessary provocation of d'Alembert's having inserted such an article on Geneva in the *Encyclopedia*. Moreover, Rousseau used the *Preface* of his *Letter to d'Alembert* to signal a public break with his long-time friend, Diderot. "I had an Aristarchus [critic] severe and just," he wrote. "I no longer have him, I no longer want one: but I shall regret him without ceasing, and I miss him more in my heart than in my writings." Then follows a quotation from *Ecclesiasticus* out of the Biblical *Apochrypha* (Book xxii, verses 26–27), emphasizing the impossibility of reconciliation. In addition, Rousseau's *Letter to d'Alembert* appeared as a further attack on the *Encyclopedia* at a most inconvenient time when it was about to be condemned and its publication stopped indefinitely by the French government.

D'Alembert wrote Rousseau a calm, polite, and reasoned reply. But Geneva did not establish a theater within its boundaries. Voltaire continued his private production of plays at Tournay and Ferney outside of Genevan jurisdiction, supported on his little stage or in the audience, by aristocratic inhabitants of the austere Swiss city. Even the English historian Gibbon attended in early days, finding Voltaire's acting too declamatory for his taste.

II   *Rousseau's Novel*, La Nouvelle Héloïse (The New Heloïse)
(1756–1761)

"I did not begin to live," wrote Rousseau in the last of his four autobiographical letters to M. de Malesherbes, Director of Publications, "until the 9th of April, 1756" (I, 1138). Soon, from his eager afternoon walks, he knew every path, every thicket, every grove of trees, every pleasant hiding place near his new home. It was a charming retreat, just made for him, it seemed (I, 403).

Now he turned over in his mind various subjects for writing. There was his great work on *Political Institutions*, which he had been meditating ever since those diplomatic days in Venice. It became in 1762 the famous *Social Contract*. There was the revision of the works of the Abbé de Saint-Pierre, soon abandoned for more original and more attractive enterprises of his own. There was a book on the *Morals of the Senses or the Wise Man's Materialism*, never completed. Then there was a treatise on Education, *Emile*, requested by Mme de Chenonceaux for use with her young son.

All these projects gradually for a time gave place in June, 1756, to quite different reveries. He was now almost forty-four years old and yet had not known an ideal enduring love such as he desired and felt himself capable of experiencing, yet here he was plunged into a sad liaison with poor Thérèse, quite unable to share his life and subtle thoughts.

Suddenly his mind flashed back twenty-five years to that delightful day of the picnic at Toune with Mlle Galley and Mlle de Graffenried. Both were charming girls, but he thought he would have preferred to be loved by the blond Mlle Galley. So he began imagining her as the heroine of what gradually became a novel told in the form of letters, an epistolary novel somewhat like, yet so different from, that popular *Clarissa Harlowe* of the English Richardson, widely read also in France in the Abbé Prévost's softened translation (1751–52). In an age almost without newspapers or colorful magazines, devoid of rapid communication by telegraph or telephone, news, thoughts, feelings transmitted themselves largely by letters. It was natural that this letter form should extend itself to the novel also.

Rousseau began to jot down on paper a few scattered letters of a blond Julie d'Etange, of her brunet friend Claire, of the hero Saint-Preux. These letters were first written by Rousseau, as they came to mind, without definite plan. Later he had great difficulty in adding connecting letters to Parts I and II and never did succeed completely.

"I must leave you, Mademoiselle, I feel it clearly," exclaims Saint-Preux at the beginning of his first letter to Julie. During the absence of her father, the Baron d'Etange, Julie's mother had chosen Saint-Preux some months before to be her daughter's tutor. The family possesses the estate of Clarens near Vevey on the northern shore of Lake Geneva.

Julie is described by Rousseau in his directions to the engraver of illustrations for his novel. He wishes her portrayed as "gentle, tender, modest, unaffected, enchanting" (II, 762). And she has indeed enchanted her tutor Saint-Preux.

Hesitant at first when she learns of his love and of his feeling that he must leave, Julie finally decides: "You may stay." But there is still wavering on her part. A series of short notes written in broken breathless phrases follows, and there are longer letters where question is piled upon question and exclamations abound. She even in one place actually calls Saint-Preux "a vile seducer" (II, 39), but does not continue in this tone.

Julie's cousin and most intimate friend, Claire, warns her of danger, but in the end Julie feels more confident. She and Saint-Preux will limit their studies together, make them deeper and more meaningful. They will not yield to their love for each other, knowing, as they do, that Julie's stern father, the Baron, when he returns from service in the army, will never consent to marriage between his one surviving daughter and a young man without rank or fortune.

Indeed, we are told much later in the story that Saint-Preux is only a substitute for his real name, which is never revealed (II, 674, n. Cf. II, 332, 417, n.). This use of a pseudonym in his case is due to prudence no doubt because of his role as the seducer of Julie and because of his embarrassment, like that of Rousseau himself, at his lowly social status.

A year passes by. The couple find themselves together in a secluded grove on the estate at Clarens without the protective presence of Claire. Saint-Preux is shaken by the bitter (*âcres*) kisses exchanged. Julie is nearly faint with emotion. Their kisses are *bitter* no doubt because the menacing image of the father obtrudes between the two lovers. So it had been with Rousseau himself and Mme d'Houdetot in a similar grove near her summer home at Eaubonne as they had kissed each other by moonlight, separated in their turn by Mme d'Houdetot's continuing devotion to the army officer and minor poet, Saint-Lambert.

How Voltaire laughed in derision at these "bitter kisses" which made no sense to him!

At length the Baron is ready to return from the wars. Julie sends Saint-Preux into temporary exile in the neighboring Swiss mountains. From the precipitous cliffs of Meillerie, Saint-Preux looks out across the Lake toward Clarens where he knows that Julie is and he almost casts himself down in suicide at the thought of his thwarted love.

Julie's father now returns. He is astonished and pleased at his daughter's extraordinary progress in her studies under the guidance of Saint-Preux, but, as for marriage with her tutor, no! The Baron has quite other plans. He will see that she marries his friend, M. de Wolmar, more than twice Julie's age. This determination hurries events to their climax.

Saint-Preux comes back to Clarens. There Julie, completely carried away, yields to his love, which is reminiscent of the famous story of Héloïse and Abélard, recently told again in popular narratives, thus leading Rousseau to his choice of a title for his novel.

During an absence of Julie's parents, the couple, with no thought now of anything but their passion, go together to a mountain chalet where they spend several days happily in a kind of unauthorized honeymoon. Julie indeed becomes pregnant, but a miscarriage saves her from discovery. Saint-Preux on his return is threatened with a duel over Julie's honor. His antagonist would be an expert English swordsman, Lord Edward Bomston. To keep Saint-Preux from a desperate choice between disgrace if he refuses to fight and wounds or possible death, if he does, Julie confesses to Lord Edward that she and Saint-Preux are in fact lovers. Lord Edward, fully siding now with the young couple, endeavors to win the Baron's consent to their marriage. All in vain. Thereupon he offers them refuge and material support on his English estate in Yorkshire, but Julie, advised in cautious general terms by Claire, decides against such exile. She will stay in her own country with her family and friends. She will marry M. de Wolmar as her father wishes, but only with Saint-Preux's consent. This he gives, signing his brief reluctant note with the letters "S. G." for which commentators give no explanation, but which we may interpret as the initials of his real name, known only to Julie, her parents, and perhaps Claire. Saint-Preux is now persuaded by Claire and Lord Edward to absent himself in Paris.

A series of letters here gives voice to Rousseau's own criticisms of the French capital. He emphasizes an attack on adultery in higher society due to the frequent "marriages of convenience," as they were called when rank and fortune were rated more important than love. Rousseau's own patrons, Mme d'Houdetot,

Mme Dupin, and Mme d'Epinay, among others, were notable examples. Rousseau also attacked in his novel French opera, French music in contrast to Italian melody, along with the luxury, the poverty, the rush and roar of the great city.

Back at Clarens, Julie's mother discovers the incriminating letters of Saint-Preux to her daughter, but the mother, not strong, becomes ill and dies not long afterward.

So Julie is married to M. de Wolmar. The solemnity of the religious ceremony makes her determined to respect her marriage vows, as she repeats them, even though she does not love M. de Wolmar.

Saint-Preux goes on a four-year voyage around the world as a member of the expedition headed by the English Admiral Anson.

Six years have passed. Julie has two young sons. Claire, after a happy marriage with a M. d'Orbe, is now a widow, the mother of a charming vivacious daughter, Henriette. By invitation, Saint-Preux returns to Clarens. Wolmar, thinking that time may have cured him of his long-ago love for Julie, plans to test him and, if possible, to make him the tutor of their children. Wolmar is depicted in a late revision of the novel as an atheist, typical of Rousseau's final plan to preach reconciliation between liberal devout people like Julie and virtuous atheists such as Wolmar. This decision on the part of the author came as a result of the government's suppression of the *Encyclopedia* in 1759. Later, Rousseau admitted in his *Dialogued Preface* to the novel that his attempt to reconcile the devout and the *philosophes* was as vain a plan as any of the well-intentioned projects of the Abbé de Saint-Pierre which Jean-Jacques had revised or contemplated revising.

Saint-Preux and Julie, with the deliberate encouragement of Wolmar, now take a pleasure trip on Lake Geneva. A storm forces them to land for safety at Meillerie on the southern shore of the Lake where Saint-Preux had experienced with redoubled force, in his winter solitude ten years before, all the pangs of his love for Julie. Julie too is deeply stirred by these reminiscences linked with the details of landscape, but she finds the strength of will to resist and triumph over her love which has not after all disappeared as Wolmar had ventured to hope it would with the passage of time. The storm passes. Julie and Saint-Preux return across the Lake to the other shore. The rhythmic sound of the oars in the oarlocks as the rowers bend to their task, the sombre reflections of the two separated lovers, evoke Lamartine's famous poem of "The Lake" more than a half-century later in 1817–1820.

Part V of the *Nouvelle Héloïse* offers a period of quiet, depicting the happy home life of Julie, M. de Wolmar, and the children at Clarens. This is Rousseau's ideal of family life as it should be lived, a family life such as he had never known, except briefly as a boy with M. and Mlle Lambercier at Bossey and in some degree with Mme de Warens at Annecy, Chambéry, and Les Charmettes.

In Part VI, Claire rejects Julie's attempt to persuade her to marry Saint-Preux. Lord Edward, similarly, following the advice of Claire and Saint-Preux, will not marry the repentant Italian courtesan, Lauretta Pisana, who retires to a convent. During an excursion to the famous castle of Chillon at the eastern end of the Lake, Julie's second son, Marcellin, falls into the water. Julie plunges in and rescues him, but becomes ill from the experience and, after several days, dies in a prolonged atmosphere of calm reflection, advice, and even preachment, leaving all around her, family, friends, and servants in deep grief. Thus the novel ends with her death and not, more conventionally, if too dramatically, with the double suicide of Julie and Saint-Preux in the waters of the Lake as Rousseau had first planned.

There are several hints that Wolmar, in accordance with Julie's devout forecast, will be converted from his atheism to religious belief.

Saint-Preux will remain at Clarens, devoting himself to the education of the children. Claire too will continue at Clarens, but, as we have seen, will not re-marry.

A plot summary is merely a bare skeleton. Deprived of the flesh and blood with which it is clothed by an able novelist, it can give only a pale idea of the work discussed. But Rousseau, having himself felt in vivid imagination and actual life, particularly with Mme de Warens and Mme d'Houdetot, many of the same emotions as his characters, makes them live again for his readers. In fact, various men and women correspondents wrote him page after page of admiring letters to ask if Julie and Saint-Preux in the *Nouvelle Héloïse* were not actually drawn from living models, as in a sense they truly were.

The epistolary form of the novel added to its cogency, putting everything, action, thoughts, and experiences, into the first person. There were limitations evidently—repetitions, as each character looked at the same events from an individual viewpoint, a longer, slower-paced narrative, an absence of the all-seeing eye of an omniscient author, thus driving Rousseau on occasion to comment on his characters in much-criticized notes at the bottom of the page. Yet on the whole, for that particular time of widespread letter writing, the epistolary form was a definite asset.

Rousseau found too in his novel opportunity to express his ideas on many contemporary subjects. We see there the religion of Julie, liberal, free from many of the limitations of orthodoxy, yet with more emotion and more conventional belief than in the author's *Profession of Faith of a Savoyard Vicar* which would soon create such an uproar with the publication of *Emile* (1762). Julie in this respect seems to have stirred up little unfavorable criticism.

Then there are Rousseau's now well-known ideas on education with his emphasis on "leçons de choses," object lessons, instead of reliance on a too abstract approach through books. There is also the depiction of a happy, informal family life, as it is centered on Julie and surrounded by children, friends, servants, passing strangers, and even visiting beggars. There is the consequent aura associated with marriage, although it may be a less than ideal marriage in its inception, such as that with the benign, but unexciting M. de Wolmar. There are Rousseau's criticisms of conventional life as it is lived in Paris or elsewhere.

Finally, there is the vivid nature description which permeates these Swiss scenes for which Rousseau had perhaps unconsciously prepared himself by a week's voyage around the Lake of Geneva in September of 1754 (I, 393 and n. 7). An important example which plays a key role in the novel is that of Meillerie on the south shore of the Lake where Rousseau and his party stopped overnight. Saint-Preux and Julie, driven by a storm, stop there too, and Saint-Preux takes a kind of painful pleasure in showing his companion the scene of his thwarted love as he had been exiled there by Julie herself ten years before. Here is the picture now in this summer season as Rousseau describes it for us.

It is a wild and solitary scene. Twenty feet away a torrent from melting snows sweeps its muddy water, sand, and stones down the mountainside. In back of us two observers rises a chain of inaccessible rocks separating the flat ground where we were standing from that part of the Alps called the Glaciers because of the constantly increasing ice which has covered it from the time of the world's beginning. On the right, black pines cast a gloomy mass of shade. To the left of the torrent rises a forest of oaks, while below stretches that immense plain of water formed from the Alps by the Lake. This it is which separates us from the rich slopes of the Vaudois country on the opposite shore, while the whole picture is crowned by the majestic summits of the Jura mountains in the background. (II, 518)

It will be noticed that this scene is described only in broad outlines as it was observed by a man who, as he tells us in the *Confessions,* was near-sighted, referring, as he does repeatedly, to "ma vue courte" (I, 37, 158, 226, 777).

While Rousseau, in winter evenings at the Hermitage, read aloud parts of the *Nouvelle Héloïse* he had composed during the day, Thérèse, unable to express herself in detail, sobbed with appreciation while her mother, the aged Mme Levasseur, more vocal if not more discriminating, repeated constantly: "Monsieur, that is very beautiful" (I, 436).

When the *Nouvelle Héloïse* appeared late in January of 1761, it rapidly became popular in Paris, in the provinces, in Switzerland, in England, in Germany, indeed all over Europe. In France Daniel Mornet has shown that, during the rest of the eighteenth century up to 1800, in number of editions, it rivaled the vogue of Voltaire's very different *Candide* which had appeared two years earlier in January, 1759. We do not of course know how many copies were contained in each edition.

The *Nouvelle Héloïse* was of great importance for Bernardin de Saint-Pierre, for Chateaubriand, and for the literary movement of Romanticism, which in France came during the first half of the nineteenth century. The poet Lamartine exclaimed: "What a book! How powerfully it is written! I am surprised that the paper itself doesn't catch fire!" (II, xix) Even realists like Balzac and Flaubert hailed the greatness of Rousseau's novel (*Ibid.*). While some parts of the *Nouvelle Héloïse* have aged and no longer move readers so powerfully today as they once did, the novel has left its profound mark and has shown other writers how to make the most of their genius in nature description, in the portrayal of emotion, and in the development of love.

III   *Rousseau and the Abbé de Saint-Pierre's* Project for Perpetual Peace *(1761)*

Among the many well-intentioned, but complex and long-winded works of the Abbé de Saint-Pierre, Rousseau, at the behest of Mme Dupin, rewrote two, but published only the second. The one unpublished was the Abbé's *Polysynodie* on the division of governmental powers among different men even in an absolute monarchy; the other was the good Abbé's hopeful *Project for Perpetual Peace*. When this *Project* appeared in its original version, the aged Cardinal Fleury, from his disillusioned vantage point as Prime Minister of France, wrote the author sarcastically that he ought first to have sent missionaries to the crowned heads of the various European powers urging them to give up narrow views of what was assumed to be self-interest in favor of the humane advantages of enduring peace (Voltaire, *Œuvres complètes*, Moland ed., XIV, 129). Rousseau, in his turn endeavored to present the Abbé de Saint-Pierre's views in a clearer, less prolix, and more convincing style. The *Project* in Rousseau's version was published in the early spring of 1761.

Voltaire, in spite of his horror at the continued blood-letting of the Seven Years' War, was not too friendly either to Rousseau or to his *Project*. He felt it still remained utterly impractical and satirized it at the end of March in 1761 under the title, *Decree of an Emperor of China* (Leigh, VIII, 282, n.).

Rousseau's own realistic *Judgment* of the *Project* he withheld until after his death, summing up his views expressively at the end of a more detailed statement: "Do not say then if his system was not adopted that it was because it was not good; say rather that it was too good to be adopted" (III, 599).

IV *The* Social Contract *(1762)*

We recall that Rousseau, while Secretary to the French ambassador at Venice in 1743–44, conceived the idea of writing a great book on *Political Institutions.* "I had seen," he said, "that everything depended very much on politics and that ... no people would ever be anything except what the nature of its government allowed it to be. Thus this great question of what is the best government possible is reduced to the following: what is the nature of the government suitable to form a people which shows itself to be the most virtuous, the most enlightened, the wisest, and in short the best in the broadest sense of the word?" (I, 404–405).

Rousseau, thinking of Geneva, thinking of France, and contrasting them in his mind with Venice, meditated on this idea and worked on it sporadically, not even discussing it with his closest friend, Diderot. Meanwhile, Montesquieu, with his great book, *The Spirit of Laws,* in 1748, came to treat some of the topics which Jean-Jacques had in mind. So in the end Rousseau extracted from his *Political Institutions* the material which formed his *Social Contract* and destroyed the rest (III, 349).

On the very first page of the *Social Contract,* Rousseau stresses his realism. He will take people as they are and laws as they can be. He rejoices that he had the good fortune to be born in a free state [Geneva] where, as one of the minority group of citizens and a member therefore of the sovereign authority, he enjoyed the right to vote and the duty to be informed.

Chapter I then opens with a characteristically striking phrase: "Man was born free," exclaims Rousseau, "and everywhere he is in chains." This sentence illustrates the author's remarkable ability to express himself in words eminently quotable and never to be forgotten. Such a sentence easily becomes a slogan of revolt and of violent protest. "If a people is forced to obey," continues Rousseau, "it does well, but as soon as it becomes able to shake off its yoke and does so, it does better." Thus the right of revolution is clearly laid down. Rousseau is ready to shock his conservative opponents from the beginning.

People talk of the "right of the strongest," but "might does

not make right." There is no right to enslave people. "To renounce one's liberty is to renounce one's status as a man." Indeed, "slavery and right are contradictory terms."

Sovereignty rests with the people. There is at least an implied
contract between government and people that the government
will rule only in the interest of the people at large. This is the
"social contract." Rousseau has proceeded with remarkably clear
and simple logic to state his case and has come thus to the end
of what he calls Book I.

The sovereignty of the people is inalienable and indivisible,
the author states in Book II. The "General Will" is the expression
of the people's sovereignty. The General Will is a difficult concept found already in Rousseau's Encyclopedia article on "Political
Economy," as also in Diderot's article in the same volume V
(1755) on "Right." This latter article is cited by Rousseau,
though it does not appear that the two friends are in entire
agreement on the concept.

The General Will is made known in a small state like Geneva
by the vote of its citizens. In a larger state, when the people
cannot assemble to debate and vote, the General Will must be
expressed by the rulers who are supposed to be guided by justice
in their government of the people. The General Will can err, but
Rousseau thinks that it does not err often. Even if it is mistaken,
it is still the General Will.

The state has the right of life or death over criminals, but a
state with many laws and many penalties for crime shows itself
as a weak and ill-governed state.

The welfare of a people is determined primarily by the liberty
and the equality which the citizens enjoy. Thus two of the three
key words of the French Revolutionary slogan already appear.

In Book III, Rousseau mentions three forms of government:
Democracy, Aristocracy, and Monarchy. The Democracy, he
says, rules through all or nearly all of the people. This type of
government is possible only in a small territory, where the mass
of the people can assemble to inform themselves, debate, and
vote their will. Obviously, such a view of democracy was determined by the slow and limited means of communication possible in Rousseau's time. It is greatly changed by the rapidity
of air travel, of telegraph, telephone, and television, even com-

munication by satellite, which make almost instant transfer of ideas possible, not within nations alone, but practically over the entire world.

The Aristocracy, according to Rousseau, places the government in the hands of only a few citizens while the Monarchy, he says, depends on the rule of a king. It remained the most common form of government in Rousseau's day, less common in ours, largely because of the changes in communication and the spread of ideas of liberty mentioned above.

There are in fact, adds Rousseau, few pure examples of these different forms of government. More commonly they are mixed, combining different aspects together.

No one form of government, says Rousseau, inspired no doubt by Montesquieu, is suitable for every country or climate, but a despotic government is never good for anybody.

Rousseau, unlike Montesquieu and Voltaire, is not here an admirer of the English government. "The English people think they are free," says Jean-Jacques, "they are very much mistaken. They are free only during an election of members of Parliament. Once these members are elected, the people are slaves, they are nothing" (III, 430). This is an extreme view evidently, but during the second half of the eighteenth century, knowledge of bribery and corruption in the English system of the time had become known in France and had produced a hostile reaction. Too high an idea of the perfection of the English government had been created in France during the first half of the century by the Huguenot refugees, by Voltaire, and by Montesquieu. After 1750, more information and a more realistic view had caused disillusion to set in. From one extreme, people humanly jumped to the other.

Rather surprisingly in view of the general title, Chapter XVI of Book III insists that governments are not actually instituted by contract. Such a contract does not exist in fact. It is only implied. It has been developed by Rousseau as a basis of argument to establish the people's rights.

Book III ends with Chapter XVIII: "Means of Preventing Usurpations in Government." Here Rousseau proposes a practical measure: "Periodic Assemblies of the Voters," preferably no doubt annually, not subject to postponement by the rulers. At these assemblies, two questions should come up automatically at the beginning.

"First: Does the sovereign people wish to continue the present form of government?"

"Second: Do the people wish to leave the administration to those now in charge?"

This approach was coming close to home as regards the Government of Geneva, where the some 1,800 male citizens out of the 24,000 population could merely vote on the nominated members of the Council of Two Hundred who in turn chose the Council of Twenty-five which actually held ruling power.

Hence the Procurator General, Jean-Robert Tronchin, promptly condemned these two proposals, and Rousseau's *Social Contract* was ordered to be "lacerated and burned." The book, much to Rousseau's surprise, was also considered subversive of the monarchy in France. Authorization to circulate it there was forbidden and the copies in bales shipped from Holland were even ordered returned unopened to the printer Marc-Michel Rey in Amsterdam. Inaccurate pirated copies, however, printed at Lyons, did gradually circulate in Paris, in the provinces of France, and in Geneva.

Book IV of the *Social Contract*, dealing with the forms of government in ancient Rome, though an object of Rousseau's keen admiration, is hardly relevant to his main subject. It constitutes largely padding to fill out the book and to offer a place for the next-to-the-last chapter, Chapter VIII of Book IV, "On Civil Religion." This chapter, without the preceding material on Roman History, had also figured in an earlier, briefer text of the *Social Contract*, which was not published (III, 336–44). The two texts on *Civil Religion* are of about the same length (ten pages), but are for the most part very different in wording, though coming to substantially the same conclusion.

"There is then," says Rousseau in his final version,

a purely civil profession of faith, the terms of which are to be passed by the sovereign people, not as religious dogmas, but as bases of sociability without which it is impossible to be a good citizen or a faithful subject. Without obliging anyone to believe them, the state may banish anyone who does not believe them, banish him, not as lacking in piety but as incapable of sincerely accepting the laws, the idea of justice, or of sacrificing, if necessary, his life for his duty. If anyone, after having recognized these dogmas, conducts himself as though he did not believe them, let him be punished with death. He has committed the greatest of crimes. He has lied in regard to the laws. (III, 468)

In spite of his immediate condemnation of intolerance, Rousseau had worked himself into an indefensible position. Though with the best of intentions, he had tried, naturally in vain, to reconcile tolerance with coercion of belief. Voltaire, in a vivid marginal comment on this passage in his copy of the *Social Contract,* lashed out fiercely: "All dogma is ridiculous, harmful. All constraint on dogma is abominable. Ordering anyone to believe is absurd. Limit yourself to ordering people to behave themselves rightly."

Thus, Rousseau, starting with emphasis on individual liberty, has ended with a strange tyranny in which an all-powerful government rules the people. In the face of the many complex problems which confront the modern world, it is tempting to have recourse constantly to a strong central government. But it can also be dangerous. We need to be equally on our guard against weakness and power, anarchy and despotism.

Rousseau himself in the end was not satisfied with his *Social Contract.* With characteristic frankness, he told Dussaulx near the end of his life: "Those who boast that they understand it all are smarter than I am. It's a book that needs to be done over, but I no longer have either the strength or the time."[1]

The path of liberty is not easy, as Rousseau's *Social Contract* unintentionally demonstrates. Yet, except for his conclusion with its emphasis upon the unfortunate Civil Religion, Rousseau had clearly outlined the essentials of democratic government for future readers.

V   Emile *(1762)*

In contrast to other great writers in France during the eighteenth century, Rousseau never had formal schooling. He was forced for the most part to educate himself. This fact led him to raise the questions repeatedly: What is the best

method of learning? Which subjects should we study by preference and which, traditionally installed in established systems
of education, are unworthy of our attention?

For a brief period of a few months, the kind Abbé de Gouvon
in Turin had taught Rousseau a little Latin, improved his knowledge of Italian, and given him suggestions on how and what to
read. His stay with Mme de Warens and his two years with M.
Lambercier at Bossey had also been of great help to him. For
the rest he had been obliged largely to depend on himself, aided
by such passing hints as he could pick up from observation of
others around him. So he read in order to fill the great void of
his ignorance. He studied because he wished to learn. His interest in education was therefore deep and intensely personal.
In the end, he wrote that few people of his age had read as
much (IV, 31). Certainly, few had read with equal profit.

It is not strange that, in a letter to his father, his thoughts
turned to being a tutor, a "gouverneur," to a young boy of
wealthy and noble family (Leigh, I, pp. 30–31). This ambition
was realized when, aided by Mme de Warens, he obtained a
position with the two older sons of a M. de Mably at Lyons.
The elder boy, M. de Sainte-Marie, was only five and a half
years old and his brother four and a half, when Rousseau first
knew them in the autumn of 1740 (I, 267, n. 7). Jean-Jacques,
thinking of the boys as he left them in 1741 and remembering
not altogether accurately, recorded in the *Confessions* that M.
de Sainte-Marie was eight or nine years old (I, 267). The
second son in his recollection would presumably have been a
year or a year and a half younger.

Rousseau held this position of tutor for only about nine months.
The two boys were difficult and Jean-Jacques, in spite of his
excellent theories, was not a firm disciplinarian. He wrote, however, a long and informative letter to the father, M. de Mably,
and a detailed *Project for the Education of M. de Sainte-Marie*
which are most revealing of Rousseau's ideas on education at
the time. Important goals were character and judgment, and not
knowledge alone. Rousseau was here partly inspired no doubt
by his favorite Montaigne, who, in his famous sixteenth-century
Essays, as we have seen, preferred "a head well formed" over
one "well filled."

Rousseau's life had therefore been one long experience in self-education. This was his background when, in 1757, he began expressing his ideas on the subject in the *Nouvelle Héloïse* through the discussions between Saint-Preux, Julie, and M. de Wolmar. Mme de Chenonceaux, daughter-in-law of Rousseau's patron, Mme Dupin, had asked him for his suggestions on education as a guide for her son. Jean-Jacques thought first of writing only a brief memoir on the subject, but his ideas grew upon him until they expanded to fill a whole volume.

Rousseau was rarely comfortable thinking his thoughts in the abstract. He had early been a dramatist though hardly a successful one. Jean-Jacques was, however, in many ways instinctively a novelist, as the *Nouvelle Héloïse* clearly shows. So, while the boy to be educated was at first only vaguely a person, gradually he became more definitely characterized and finally, rather late in the process of composition, took on a name, Emile. Thus a kind of educational novel was born.

The Englishman, John Locke, had published his book *On Human Understanding* in 1690. It was translated into French ten years later. Furthermore, Locke's treatise *On the Education of Children,* dating from 1693, had already been utilized by Rousseau in his *Project for the Education of M. de Sainte-Marie.* There was also much writing on education in France and Jean-Jacques had read widely on the subject. Thus he was by no means ill prepared to discuss it himself.

From the beginning Rousseau wants the child to be physically active. He does not approve of his limbs being bound by the restrictive *maillot,* in swaddling clothes, as was the custom of the time. In Russia a half-century ago it was possible in the summer to witness striking examples of the old and the new in this respect on the streets and in the big city parks almost side by side.

Rousseau further opposes having the child put out to nurse, as was the widespread custom among the aristocracy in the eighteenth century. Infant mortality was frightfully high in any case, and was increased by unsanitary conditions in the country among these peasant nurses. Besides, they were commonly illiterate and kept no records so that it was often uncertain which children died and which returned home. It has been estimated that not more than one out of twenty survived (IV, 273, n.1).

Rousseau, it will be remembered, had abandoned the five children he had had with Thérèse and put them in the Paris foundling asylum. He came finally to feel deep remorse for this irretrievable act; a remorse increased, evidently, as he reflected over the problems of *Emile*.

Education, said Rousseau, should follow nature. The first education, he held, should be negative. The basic problem is to lose time, not to gain it. There is no aim to develop an infant prodigy. Emile should form ideas only as fast as he can understand them. Rousseau does not want the child to speak glibly in words without meaning for him. He will learn by experience, by object lessons, by "leçons de choses," more than from books.

Thus private property which Jean-Jacques had fiercely condemned in his *Discourse on Inequality* as contrary to the state of nature, he now defends in *Emile* as necessary to society. Emile and his tutor plant beans in a convenient plot of ground which they cultivate and tend together. They watch the beans with delight as they come up and grow and thrive. Unfortunately, they have not first consulted Robert, the gardener, who suddenly appears, pulls up their intruding beans, and tells them he had already planted there the seeds of some rare melons which had been given him. Thus Rousseau teaches the rights of property when it is already devoted to legitimate and enlightened use. It is a hard lesson for Emile, but effective.

Shall Emile learn the catechism? No, because it is full of concepts he cannot understand. Shall he be taught ideas of morality and virtue? Only gradually as he grows to appreciate their meaning. How shall he find his way back home from a walk in the country? By observing the position of the sun in the sky when he sets out and allowing for the change several hours later when he returns.

Shall he learn religion early? No, because it is beyond his years. But, in the Fourth Book of *Emile*, the *Profession of Faith of a Savoyard Vicar* reflects the teachings of the Abbé Gaime in Turin and of the Abbé Gâtier in Savoy as given to Jean-Jacques himself and recounted in the *Confessions*. We see also in this

Profession Rousseau's own ideas frankly and even dangerously expressed. Indeed, it was particularly this *Profession of Faith* that caused the book *Emile* to be promptly "lacerated and burned" both at Paris and Geneva, sending Rousseau into years of wandering exile.

Rousseau himself holds to a simplified Christianity, a Christianity without miracles, a Christianity of good conduct inspired by the principles of Jesus. Rousseau believes in God the Supreme Being. He does not hold to the orthodox doctrine of *Hors de l'Eglise, point de salut*—"Outside of the Church, no salvation." He does not believe in Hell fire and Damnation. He is, in short, as Lanson has pointed out, a liberal Protestant creating a new and independent Protestantism of his own.[2]

So there is much in *Emile* to inspire a more interesting and more effective system of education. But we must not in all cases follow Rousseau literally. We should rather take general inspiration from his book, avoid his excesses, and profit from his suggestions. Some writers have thought that Rousseau wished to make education easy. Instead, he realized that learning is difficult and must remain so. Punishments should fit the crime. When Emile breaks a window pane, the damage is not repaired for several days, the wind and the rain come in, Emile catches cold, and learns the hard way—but learns—that windows are not to be broken.

Emile is a book to be read for its total inspiration. It is not to be followed too closely in details. Above all, it stresses the importance of the human element in education, more significant than equipment or fine buildings, desirable as these may be. *Emile* depicts an ideal which can never be completely realized. Only royal families or the very wealthy can afford an individual teacher for each pupil, and even that, depriving the young of associations with their contemporaries of similar age and interests, offers serious disadvantages. But *Emile* remains one of the key books of modern times. It has inspired Pestalozzi, Montessori, John Dewey, and other great leaders in educational theory during the nineteenth and twentieth centuries. It is a book to be read and pondered carefully.

Book V of *Emile* is entitled *Sophie or about Women.* It depicts the character and traits of the girl who is to become Emile's wife, since, as Rousseau says, quoting the Biblical book of *Genesis*, "it is not good for man to be alone." Sophie, named obviously after Sophie d'Houdetot, is actually shown more completely as a person than is Emile. Rousseau evidently took special pleasure in portraying her.

Sophie's parents have been rich, but, falling upon difficult days, they have abandoned the dangerous whirlpool of Paris for simpler and more natural life in the country. They are, however, good and wise. They will advise Sophie about her marriage, but they will allow her to choose her husband with love as a basis.

Emile is a boy of one favorite book, Defoe's *Robinson Crusoe*. Sophie's book is Archbishop Fénelon's *Télémaque* (1699), an educational novel written for the instruction of the Dauphin, heir to the French throne. Sophie in fact became so enchanted with the story that she actually fell in love with the fictional hero, Telemachus, the son of Ulysses, and for a time could not bring herself even to look at contemporry suitors, much to her father's amused raillery. Rousseau realized that he had set out on a false route, but, with charming naïveté, refrained from eliminating this part of the story. Instead, he merely let it stand, acknowledged his mistake, and embarked once more on his intended course.

Emile goes with his tutor in search of Sophie, finds her, falls in love, takes lodgings in a neighboring village, and pays his court to her. He gradually wins her love, though there are occasional realistic manifestations of moodiness, coquetry, or temper on the part of Sophie.

The tutor prudently believes that the durability of the love of these two young people should be tested. After all, Sophie is only seventeen, Emile about twenty-one. So Emile and his "gouverneur" depart on a two-year journey through France and other unspecified countries. Emile will try to discover whether some other government is better and offers a happier place to live. To that end, Rousseau rather tediously incorporates in his book the main principles of his *Social Contract* which, we remember, had already been denied entry into France and would shortly be condemned in Geneva.

Finally, Emile returns, decides that he may as well continue to live in France, imperfect though it is, and he marries Sophie. The tutor gives the couple frank and sound advice on how to maintain their marriage on a democratic basis, equally fair to both sides, making for the continued happiness of husband and wife.

Modern critics have found the education of Sophie even more than that of Emile, too lacking in intellectual content. Rousseau, in fact, was less liberal toward women than Archbishop Fénelon, whose book on the *Education of Girls* preceded Rousseau's *Emile* by three quarters of a century. Jean-Jacques, in this respect, lagged behind Montesquieu and especially Voltaire.

D'Alembert, however, in a letter to Mlle de Lespinasse (Leigh, XI, A274–75), praised this Book V of *Emile* highly. He wrote that he had read it with special pleasure. The reason lay in the vivid characterization of Sophie and the evident enjoyment Rousseau manifested in drawing the picture of her virtues and foibles, her sudden changes of mood and impulse.

VI   Emile and Sophie, or the Solitaries

Rousseau too must have had a special affection for this Book V with its realistic portrayal of Sophie. He could not abandon it. So, promptly in 1762, he evidently used his few spare moments to begin a sequel entitled *Emile and Sophie, or the Solitaries.* This narrative consists of forty-four printed pages, divided into two letters by Emile to his tutor. The first letter is the longer, comprising thirty-one pages; the second, unfinished, is contained in the remaining thirteen. Rousseau read these two "letters" on November 22, 1762, to his friend Kirchberger (Leigh, XIV, 75).[3]

In this sequel Rousseau set out to test Emile and Sophie to see how well they endure misfortune. Sophie's parents die. Shortly after this loss of her parents, Sophie's second child, a daughter, falls victim to the high infant mortality of the time, and the young mother is unable to control her grief. To afford her change and diversion, Emile moves with her from the country to Rousseau's hated city, Paris. But there, Emile, in spite of his tutor's previous warning, is caught up in the social whirl and more and more neglects his wife, Sophie. Sophie is unfaithful and becomes pregnant by her seducer. With bitter self-condemnation, she confesses her fault, but Emile is beside himself with shock and grief. In a mad burst of physical activity he runs and walks about the big city, not knowing where he is going until, utterly exhausted by over-exercise and lack of food, he falls down somewhere and sleeps. When he awakes, he is calmer. He eats, goes into the country and takes a job as a carpenter in a shop. The boss recognizes him as an excellent workman. He is recognized also as a *monsieur*, not a mere *compagnon* or fellow-worker. He muses. Shall he take from Sophie the boy, the one child who is theirs together? Sophie comes and from the door observes him there working, but does not reveal herself and is not seen by Emile. Emile decides, it is best to leave the boy with his mother.

Emile, like Rousseau, will go into exile, but his exile will be voluntary. He sets out alone and on foot across the countryside, making his way gradually south to Marseille and working from time to time at his skilled trade of carpentry, as financial need demands. At Marseille, he takes ship to Naples, then boards another boat for an unknown destination on the Mediterranean. The captain of this second vessel, installing a magnet secretly in the compass (memory of an incident in *Emile*, IV, 437–40), causes it to deviate so that he delivers them all, passengers and crew, into the hands of Barbary pirates as slaves in Algiers. Emile kills the treacherous captain, but, worked to desperation by a pirate overseer, leads a successful revolt, is himself chosen as a more reasonable overseer, and becomes a favorite of the Dey of Algiers. Here the narrative suddenly stops. Rousseau was eager to complete it, but—his time filled with the *Confessions*, the *Dialogues*, and the *Reveries*—was never able to do so. This outcome, as it turned out, was fortunate. He recounted his varied plans to several friends including especially Bernardin de Saint-Pierre. Rousseau's story of Emile and Sophie, largely realistic up to this point, even in the part dealing with the pirates of Algiers, was suddenly to have taken a wildly romantic and impossible turn, surpassing even the adventures of Prévost's *Cleveland* (1731–39), read earlier with such fascination by Rousseau (I, 220 and n.1). In fact, it would seem to have been a kind of throw-back to those improbable tales read in early boyhood until all hours of the night in company with his too permissive father. It is most fortunate that Rousseau did not finish his literary career in this way where it in a sense began. It would not have added to his reputation, but quite the reverse, would have taken from it.

What he did complete of the two "letters" ranks as one of his most impressive brief works. The reader, once he has started it, finds it hard to put the book down. It is a convincing study of pain, frustration, and passion, combined with those physical reactions associated no doubt with Rousseau's *Materialism of the Sage* which also he never completed. The part we have is sufficient to reflect clearly the author's sufferings as he endured the censorship of *Emile* and began his own years of exile.

These two so-called "letters" were published in 1780, after the author's death. They deserve to be better known than they generally are, but we can be glad that fate in this case was kind and did not permit Rousseau to go further.

CHAPTER 4

Years of Controversy (1762–1770)

I   *Rousseau's Letter to M. de Saint-Germain (1770)*

ROUSSEAU did not know M. de Saint-Germain, but, feeling the need of someone to confide in, he asked permission to make his acquaintance and to write him. M. de Saint-Germain readily agreed and Rousseau wrote him a long letter on February 26, 1770.

This communication is much more than an ordinary letter. It is twenty-nine printed pages in the *Correspondance générale*, more than ten pages longer than Rousseau's famous letter to Voltaire on Providence. The letter to M. de Saint-Germain ranks, then, as a work apart. It is filled with Rousseau's mental disturbance over the plot which he feels has been organized against him, a plot in which the Duc de Choiseul, Minister of France, Grimm, Diderot, and d'Holbach are thought to be leaders. Later even Rousseau's old friend Duclos, in whom he had had great confidence, comes under his suspicion. To a lesser degree, Jean-Jacques begins to wonder, no doubt unjustly, about Mme de Luxembourg. After the failure of Rousseau's English journey with Hume, Mme de Boufflers draws a hostile footnote. Without agreeing with Rousseau's mad concept of an organized plot against him, we cannot fail to perceive the unwavering hostility by this time of Grimm, Diderot, d'Holbach, and Mme d'Epinay with her doctored *Memoirs*. We can sympathize strongly with Rousseau who felt himself utterly alone in face of such intense, if not always concerted hostility.

II   *Four Letters to M. de Malesherbes (January, 1762)*

M. de Malesherbes, Director of French Publications, had been most gracious to Rousseau. Though obligated to enforce censorship, this eighteenth-century nobleman was at heart liberal and, if he had been permitted, would have come close to allowing the free expression of ideas. In fact, he had strangely believed that Rousseau's *Emile*, bold though it was in its religious tenets, could actually be printed and circulated in the France of his time without interference. In this opinion, as it happened, he was grievously mistaken, most unhappily for Rousseau.

M. de Malesherbes wrote Rousseau a letter on Christmas day, 1761, stressing his belief that the causes of Jean-Jacques's melancholy were chiefly physical and advising him to make them known to the public in explanation of his surprising preference for a life of solitude in the country.

Rousseau replied to M. de Malesherbes in a series of four letters, dated January 4, 12, 26, and 28, 1762, which are of great importance from the standpoint of self-revelation (Leigh, X, 4–9, 24–29, 52–58, and 63–68).

In the first letter Jean-Jacques says that he was born with a love of solitude and a marked preference for the beings created by his own imagination over the people he actually met in the world about him. It was in Paris that he was unhappy, he wrote, in contrast to the independence of life in the country where his desire to do as he pleases can have free reign.

The second letter, that of January 12, recounts the famous "crisis of Vincennes," the sudden revelation out of which came Rousseau's *Discourse on the Arts and Sciences* (1751). This letter is in some ways more detailed than the later *Confessions*. It is in part familiar to the readers of this book in connection with the composition of the *First Discourse*. The letter is especially notable for its emphasis on the physical reactions which accompanied Rousseau's emotions. He stresses that this experience was the beginning of his great system of natural goodness, embodied in three works: his *First Discourse* (1751), the *Discourse on Inequality* (1755), and *Emile* (1762). The success of his *First Discourse* was the beginning of Rousseau's fame, of his "reform," and of his setting himself up as a copiest, particularly of music.

The third letter dates from January 26. It recounts his joy at being established in the country at the Hermitage by Mme d'Epinay. This letter narrates also his delight in long afternoon walks accompanied only by his dog. It was his practice to eat an early mid-day dinner and to slip away as soon as possible in order to avoid undesired visitors who might prevent him from leaving.

The final letter is of January 28. It contains a reference to Diderot's wounding thrust about a citizen "living alone," which signaled the tragic break in their long friendship. This letter explains that Rousseau would not have been able to live and write freely in a Geneva inhabited by Voltaire. Indeed, in Geneva Jean-Jacques could not have published the dedication of his *Discourse on Inequality*.

Moreover, it is impossible for him to write merely as a professional author. That is why he had declined M. de Malesherbes's offer of a generous regular stipend in return for contributing a few book reviews every month to the *Journal des Savants*. He can write only when moved by a deep conviction, when he is persuaded of the truth and signal importance of what he is writing.

Rousseau cannot conceal his violent aversion toward those ranks of society which dominate others. "I hate the great," he exclaims in a sudden burst of anger. "I hate their caste, their harshness, their prejudices, their pettiness, and their vices, and I would hate them more if I despised them less."

Then with a sudden marked change in tone, he continues: "In my dreams I have many times supposed M. de Luxembourg not a Duke, but a Marshall of France, a good country gentleman living in an old château, and Jean-Jacques Rousseau, not an author of books, but a man of average mind and a little more,[1] presenting himself to the Lord and Lady of the castle, pleasing them, finding in their company life's happiness and contributing to theirs; if to make the dream more attractive, you will allow me with my shoulder to push the Malesherbes castle half a league away from there, it seems to me, Monsieur, that with such a dream, I shouldn't wish to wake up for a long time."

With this graceful tempering of his fierce tirade against the great of society, Rousseau concludes his letter and the series.

Never, he said, had he written more easily. Perhaps only half realizing it at the moment, he had already begun his *Confes-*

sions, the autobiography which Marc-Michel Rey, his publisher at Amsterdam, had for some time been urging upon him.

III Rousseau's Letter to Christophe de Beaumont, Archbishop of Paris (1763)

Rousseau headed his letter "Jean-Jacques Rousseau, Citizen of Geneva, to Christophe de Beaumont, Archbishop of Paris, Duke of St. Cloud, Peer of France, Commander of the Order of the Holy Spirit, Director of the Sorbonne, etc." (IV, 925). It is a striking contrast, but Voltaire, in a marginal comment, condemned it as a buffoonery. He himself on occasion enjoyed parading his titles: "Lord of Ferney, Lord of Tournay, Gentleman in Ordinary of the King's Bedchamber, Member of the French Academy, etc."

Rousseau tells us in the *Confessions* that he had great personal respect for M. de Beaumont because of his constancy in defending his opinions against King Louis XV and the Parlement, even to the point of prolonged exile in the provinces (IV, 931, n. 3) (cf. I, 606).

The Archbishop's charge to his diocese was dated August 20, issued August 28, 1762. Rousseau did not receive it until September 26 at Môtiers-Travers (IV, p. clxxi). He immediately decided on a reply and started to work on it. His answering letter is dated November 18, 1762, but it was not sent to his printer Rey at Amsterdam until January 1, 1763 and was published in March of that year (IV, clxxi).

Since Rousseau's religious ideas are already familiar to us from the *Profession of Faith of a Savoyard Vicar* in *Emile,* we need not dwell upon them here. The main point, as we have seen before, is that Rousseau regards himself as a follower of Christ, hence a Christian, without the necessity of believing in a specific doctrine such as is laid down by the Archbishop.

"If the life and the death of Socrates are of a sage, the life and death of Jesus are those of a God," says Rousseau (IV, 993). His divinity consists in the memory of his life and death. "I confess," he said, "that the majesty of the Scriptures astounds me; the sacredness of the Gospels speaks to my heart" (IV, 992).

Rousseau still wrestles with the problem of "civil religion,"

which he considers necessary to make one follow natural law.
He had struggled with it in his *Letter to Voltaire on Providence*,
in his *Social Contract*, in *Emile*, and now here in his *Letter
to M. de Beaumont*. But the problem of reconciling his civil
religion and its severe sanctions of banishment or death with
tolerance still remained impossible.

Finally, Rousseau comes to a challenging conclusion: "You
have called me impious," he says to the Archbishop:

> You call me an imposter. . . . My Lord, you have insulted me publicly.
> I have just proved that you have subjected me to calumny. If you
> were a private citizen like me, I could have you cited before a court
> of justice before which we would both appear, I with my book and
> you with your charge, and you would certainly be found guilty and
> condemned to make me a reparation as public as the offense has
> been. But you hold a rank which dispenses you from being just,
> and I am nothing. However, you who profess the Gospel, you a
> prelate placed to teach others their duty, you know what your duty
> is in such a case. As for me, I have done mine, I have nothing more
> to say to you, and I keep silence.
>
> Deign, my Lord, to accept my profound respect. J.J. Rousseau.
> At Môtiers, the 18 November, 1762. (IV, 1006, 1007)

With eighty printed pages, Rousseau's letter seems long
today. He was obliged, however, to quote frequently at length
from *Emile*, partly because the Archbishop had given only the
negative portions, omitting positive passages which were more
favorable to Rousseau's ideas. Jean-Jacques did not of course
expect to convince M. de Beaumont or induce a retraction on
his part. He did, however, hope to enlighten many neutral or
friendly readers in Geneva as well as in France and by his
quotations make up for the lack of copies of *Emile* itself after
its immediate suppression in both countries.

IV *Rousseau's* Letters Written from the Mountain *(1764)*

It will be recalled that, according to d'Alembert (*Mélanges*,
II, 360), Geneva, in the middle of the eighteenth century, was a
city of some 24,000 persons. Only about 1,800 of those men of
twenty-five years of age or older had the rank of *citizens* and

enjoyed the right to vote. They constituted the General Council. The rest, *natives, inhabitants,* and *subjects,* were without voice in the government. Even the *citizens,* however, could vote only for candidates already proposed for the Council of Two Hundred, which in turn chose the chief governing body, the Council of Twenty-five. Thus Geneva was much less of a democracy than it had appeared to Rousseau at the time of the fulsome praise he had lavished on it in his dedication of the *Discourse on Inequality* in 1754 and 1755. In 1707 and in 1735 serious revolts of the Citizens had sought more power, but without notable success. Moreover, the watchful eye of the French monarchy, the most powerful of the three "mediators," also favored aristocratic control of Geneva by the small Council of Twenty-five.

This was the situation when the Procurator General, Jean-Robert Tronchin, as the voice of Geneva's government, published anonymously his able *Letters Written from the Country* in 1763. Rousseau answered them in his *Letters Written from the Mountain* of 1764, the mountain in this case being the high ground of Môtiers-Travers where for the time being he had found refuge from the severe condemnation of *Emile* in France and Geneva.

The first three of these *Letters from the Mountain* deal chiefly with the defense of the religious ideas in *Emile,* so necessary after its confiscation and the difficulty in obtaining any but inaccurate pirated copies printed in Lyons. The fourth and fifth letters center on the illegal procedure by which Geneva had condemned the *Social Contract* and *Emile* (Wade, *FR,* May, 1976, pp. 933). The sixth letter points out that the *Social Contract* had been burned only at Geneva where it was not printed (III, 810). The seventh letter notes that the Little Council, the Council of Twenty-five, has now become supreme. Geneva is thus at the mercy of "twenty-five despots" (III, 835). In the eighth letter, we see that the right of representation, established in 1707 and reaffirmed in 1735 is intended to protect the rights of citizens. The ninth and concluding letter indicates that Rousseau has been studying the English government. He finds that the King of England actually has less power than Geneva's Little Council. The great need now of Geneva is peace and harmony among all its citizens. It is on this note that Rousseau, who has resigned his citizenship, concludes.

The *Letters Written from the Mountain* are clear, interesting, and forcefully written. They rank as one of Rousseau's most powerfully controversial works. Their central aim, as Wade has pointed out (*op. cit.*), is more democracy for Geneva. The letters do not, however—and this is perhaps natural under the circumstances—propose to extend this democracy beyond the limited body of those classified as *citizens* to include a majority of the permanent inhabitants. The need for that had not yet become clear to Rousseau.

V   *Rousseau's Interest in Corsica and Poland*

The rejection of Rousseau's *Social Contract* (1762) in France and in Geneva made him many violent enemies, but won him also some friends.

The Mediterranean island of Corsica had long been misruled by Italian Genoa. Several Corsican leaders, along with the young Englishman Boswell on the Grand Tour, sought out Rousseau's ideas of an independent government for the island. The result took form as Rousseau's *Project of a Constitution for Corsica,* completed in September, 1765 (III, p. ccvii), but not published during the author's lifetime. The whole question became moot, however, when a treaty of Versailles on May 15, 1768, made Corsica a part of France (III, p. ccviii) and an unknown infant born the following year, Napoleone Buonaparte, became a French citizen.

Poland likewise had long been a problem state. With no natural boundaries to the east or west, it was in constant danger of being swallowed up by Russia or by Germany or by both of these strong neighbors at the same time. Once more Rousseau's advice was sought. In consequence, he wrote his *Considerations on the Government of Poland,* which were completed in June of 1771 (III, p. ccxvii). Again there was no opportunity to test Rousseau's ideas by putting them into effect, but they do have the special interest of marking another effort on his part to adapt his thinking to an important contemporary problem, and one in which he remained quite independent of the *Social Contract.*

VI *Rousseau's* Confessions *(1765–1770)*

During the next years, Rousseau was chiefly occupied with writing the story of his life, a story which became his famous *Confessions.* Since Jean-Jacques, in confessing himself, felt authorized, rightly or wrongly, to confess also the supposed or real faults of others with whom he was closely involved, as for example, Mme de Warens, Mme d'Epinay, Mme d'Houdetot, Diderot, and Grimm, he realized from the beginning that he could not publish the book during his lifetime. So it came about that the first half, Books I–VI, appeared in July 1782, four years after the author's death. The second half, Books VII–XII, narrating Rousseau's life through 1765 (I, p. xxxiv), was not printed until November, 1789, on the eve of the French Revolution.

In a preliminary draft of an introduction to his book, Rousseau had made mention of his great sixteenth-century predecessor, Montaigne, author of the world-famous *Essays.* Rousseau describes Montaigne as at the head of those persons "falsely sincere," who reveal only their "amiable faults" (I, 1149–50). In his final introductory page, however, Rousseau, omitting any reference to Montaigne as a predecessor, is briefer, but still more challenging. He writes as follows:

I am forming an enterprise without previous example and which will be without an imitator. I wish to show my fellowmen a man in all the truth of nature and this man will be myself.

Myself alone. I know my heart and I know men. I am not made like any of those whom I have seen; I dare to believe that I am not like any who exist. If I am not better, at least I am different. If nature did well or ill to break the mould in which I was cast, you can judge only after reading me.

Let the trumpet of the last judgment sound when it will, I will come with this book in my hand to present myself before the Sovereign Judge. I will say boldly: this is what I have done, this is what I have thought, this is what I was. I have told the good and the bad with the same frankness. I have not kept silent over anything bad, have added nothing to the good, and if I have chanced to employ any further ornament in my text, it has been only to fill a gap due to my lack of memory. I may have supposed to be true what I knew could have been so, never what I knew to be false. I have shown myself as I was, contemptible and vile when that is what I was, good, generous, sublime when I could be so characterized. I have revealed my inner self just as you, my supreme judge, have seen it yourself. Eternal Being, gather about me the innumerable crowd of my fellow men; let them listen to my *Confessions*, let them groan over my afflictions, blush at my shortcomings. Let each of them in his turn uncover his soul at the foot of your throne with the same sincerity and then let a single one of them say, if he dare: I was better than that man. (1, 5)

In telling his story, Rousseau enjoys recovering his past, particularly the remote past of his youth. He remembers details of costume, weather, and conversation. He recreates the scenes for us, who read today. It was so that he had to tell them in order to satisfy himself as he relived the happenings of his past life. Occasionally, as we have seen him admit, he has indeed been obliged to invent minor details. These were cases where, without written records, he found himself unable to recall the complete setting. There has been no falsification here, he believes. He has told nothing but what he thought might have been true. In any case, the *Confessions* have rightly been subjected to the most careful scrutiny. They have been corrected by able critics where any correction has appeared necessary or possible with the additional information we now have.

Rousseau, as we have seen, spends much time on his early life and boyhood. Realizing that "the child is father to the man," he dwells at length upon these crucial formative years. We know little from this point of view about the early life of Montesquieu or of Voltaire. Even Diderot has not told us much about his boyhood in Langres or in Paris. We are not sure whether he attended the Collège Louis-le-Grand or the Collège d'Harcourt or perhaps both. We are uncertain about who were his professors.

In 1770 and 1771, the author gave readings of later parts of his *Confessions*, still unpublished, before groups in or near Paris. He as well as his audience, showed extraordinary endurance. In one instance, Rousseau read aloud from nine in the morning until three hours after midnight (Guéhenno, II, 247), with only brief pauses for rest and refreshment. Mme d'Epinay, indignant at Rousseau's attacks, persuaded the Lieutenant of

Police, Sartine, to stop further readings, and Mme d'Epinay, Diderot, and Grimm prepared their replies.

If Rousseau was disappointed in the reaction of these audiences to his reading, this was due no doubt to a combination of shock at his revelations and exhaustion from the unbearable length of these sessions. Who, after such an experience, could wish for anything but to go home to bed?

Without our excusing Rousseau on the ground that he has thus laid bare his soul, we have to take his remarkable frankness into consideration as we compare him with contemporaries who have not thus revealed their own inner selves.

In our account here of Rousseau's life, we have naturally drawn much on his *Confessions* which are therefore in part familiar to the reader. Rousseau's *Confessions* may rightly be called his best novel. This is said in no invidious sense of criticism. We mean only that he tells his story, not abstractly, but with those concrete and visual details which constituted the background of his thought and action. Thus he makes these events come alive again for the reader. It is a fascinating, at times almost a poetic narrative, one of surpassing interest. We share the author's inner life as well as the outer accompaniments of his movements.

Since Rousseau's *Confessions* no good biographer can ignore the early years of parentage, of friends or enemies, of play, and of schooling, which establish the foundations of habit, temperament, and the ideas of later life. In these, as in many other respects, Rousseau's *Confessions* are a very modern book. After him, Bernardin de Saint-Pierre, Rousseau's friend of his later years, tells us his story. Chateaubriand narrates his colorful *Mémoires d'Outre-Tombe.* Vigny, Hugo, Delacroix, and Baudelaire follow these examples of their predecessors. So it has been with many others, not only in France, but in England, Germany, America, and elsewhere. The example of Rousseau has been pervasive.

Obviously, Rousseau has been at times guilty of special pleading. He has admitted that he told his story in self-defense. None of his repeated efforts can excuse the abandonment of his five children to the Paris foundling asylum where they disappeared forever. Gradually, as he wrote *Emile,* his remorse grew, but it was too late. He could not retrace his steps.

The *Confessions* tell us much about Rousseau's reading. We do not of course learn all, but we have a record of many of those authors and books which shaped his personality and life. Because of his enforced self-education, this account is more complete and more significant than it otherwise would have been. He did not read under compulsion. He read largely what he wanted to read. He read in order to learn and to know.

No account is more vivid than the *Confessions.* We retrace Rousseau's steps with him. His hopes and fears become ours as well. His life endures beyond his time and extends from the eighteenth century on into the centuries following which are our own.

CHAPTER 5

Final Works (1770–1778)

I *The* Dialogues: Rousseau Judge of Jean-Jacques *(1776)*

ROUSSEAU wrote the three *Dialogues* slowly over a period of four years, while continuing to carry on his copying of music by which every morning he earned his daily living at the rate of ten cents a page. According to his records he copied more than 6,000 pages of music in six years (I, 831). Another later estimate actually runs to nearly 12,000 pages of varied material in seven years (I, p. lxviii and p. 1685, n. 3), all this by a man who professed himself lazy and disinclined to effort. Actually, he enjoyed this routine work which required no original thought.

The best explanation that Rousseau, in his mental disturbance, can find for the troubles that beset him from without lies in the theory of a general concerted plot against him. But such an organized plot, real or not, does not prevent him from arguing ably his case against a Frenchman whom he imagines as his antagonist. This Frenchman admits that he has not read Rousseau for himself. He has merely accepted as true the opinions of others who have told him for example that Rousseau did not know enough music to compose his very popular operetta *Le Devin du village*. Rousseau replied that it took only a certain taste and ear for music to write his operetta, and these it was well known that he possessed through other shorter musical pieces recognized as his. What really took knowledge was the articles and definitions on music he had written and given to Diderot at his request in 1749 for the *Encyclopedia*. Diderot shortly had turned these over to d'Alembert in 1751 for publication in that great work (I, 680, footnote). This remark explains the uncertainty whether it was Diderot who requested the articles, as the *Confessions* state (I, 348), or d'Alembert, accord-

113

ing to the opinion of the Pléiade edition of Rousseau (I, cvi).
Never in a court of justice is an indictment accepted without
hearing the accused in his own defense. But Rousseau has not
been heard. Convinced by Rousseau's serried argument, the
Frenchman agrees that he will read Rousseau's works for himself to see what they contain. This is the end of *Dialogue I*.

In the *Second Dialogue*, the Frenchman begins by saying he
has concluded that Rousseau is not virtuous since virtue comes
only from effort (I, p. 773). He is sometimes good, that is, he
aspires to goodness, but for the most part he is neutral, neither
one nor the other (p. 823).

Rousseau detests his later portraits, particularly that by Ram-
say, obtained in England by Hume, which, Rousseau believes,
makes him look like a satyr. Only his early portrait by La Tour
in 1753 is to his taste (I, p. 781). Rousseau is not a handsome
man. He is short and looks shorter because of his habit of bend-
ing his head forward. He is near-sighted. His eyes are deep-set,
his features show his age, but he is no monster (I, pp. 777–778);
his teeth are horrible, a detail included in the first draft of the
Confessions then eliminated, perhaps because it was not true
in his youth (I, 48, n. 1; p. 777, n. 5).

Rousseau does not flee from mankind out of hatred, but
from fear of what men may do to him. Diderot's phrase: "Only
the evil man is alone," is absurd and false (I, 789). The *Letter
to d'Alembert*, the *Nouvelle Héloise*, *Emile*, the *Social Contract*,
and other works are the fruit of his withdrawal to the country.
Rousseau doubts whether anyone has meditated more and written more in such a short time.

He has walked as much as six miles to listen to the nightingale
at its best. He likes simple meals, a single plate, with good wine
(I, 807–808). We know from the *Confessions* of his preference
for *Robinson Crusoe* (I, 812) and of his continued enjoyment
of Plutarch (I, 819). He used to read La Calprenède's *Cas-
sandra*, d'Urfé's *Astrée*, and the older novels (I, 819). The
success of his *First Discourse* in 1751 plunged him into writing
(I, 828–29). We recognize this as an old thesis of Rousseau's.
In fact, however, he had been writing hopefully for years in his
youth, though without success.

His accident on the streets of Paris, recounted later in the

Second Revery, showed people not coming to his aid (I, 882; cf. 1005). Yet he was mourned by the English when he left Wootten.

There is now another reference to the frankness of his *Confessions* (I, 902–903). We see the friendship which he enjoys with George Keith, "My Lord Marshall," as he was currently called (I, 901; cf. 864). Then follows a further passage on Rousseau's musical abilities (I, 872–873; cf. 181, n. 1), and here the *Second Dialogue* ends.

The *Third Dialogue* begins with the Frenchman's return from a somewhat extended stay in the country. He has not been bored, for he has occupied his time with reading Rousseau. The Frenchman quotes numerous passages to show that Rousseau has violently criticized men of letters, doctors,[1] kings, the great and the rich in society, women, and even the English, who are said to be not as free as they think they are when they elect representatives to Parliament. How can Rousseau have failed to expect attacks from all sides when he has thus made himself the enemy of nearly everybody of influence?

Rousseau answers that he has not been surprised, but he attributes these attacks on him primarily to a plot, led by the Duc de Choiseul, minister of foreign affairs, who misunderstood as hostile a passage written by Rousseau, and to the machinations of Jean-Jacques's one-time friend Grimm, now become his ardent enemy.

But the Frenchman finds Rousseau's doctrine "simple and sane" (I, 930). His work is made up of the meditations of a man solitary, passionate, enamoured of virtue, liberty, and order (I, 932). His point of view has been developed gradually. One must follow it progressively through his works. Rousseau is primarily the "man of nature." He is opposed to sudden revolutions (I, 935). He is innocent and virtuous in that sense. All he wants is for his innocence to be reestablished in spite of the plot against him (I, 976).

The *Third Dialogue* is followed by what Rousseau entitles the *History of this Writing,* explaining how he tried unsuccessfully to place a copy of his *Dialogues* one Saturday on the altar of the Cathedral of Notre-Dame in Paris. For the first time in forty-six years in the capital city, he had found the gates of

the altar closed. After this rebuff, he put the manuscript in the
hands of an old friend, Condillac. The latter evidently considered it only another writing of Rousseau's and suggested
some revisions and some changes in order. Rousseau would have
none of this, but left his manuscript and gradually ceased having
any more relations with Condillac. Rousseau also put a copy in
the hands of a young Englishman, Boothby, who guarded it
faithfully and took it with him to England.

Finally, the manuscript of the *Dialogues* was published four
years after Rousseau's death by Moultou and Du Peyrou in 1782
along with the first half of the *Confessions.*

In sum, in spite of Rousseau's mad obsession with an organized plot against him, the *Dialogues* show him a complete
master of his argument. In this respect, the *Dialogues* are
revealing and are somewhat less sad than they have often
appeared to readers of Rousseau.

II   *The* Reveries of the Solitary Walker *(1776–1778)*

After the three *Dialogues: Rousseau Judge of Jean-Jacques,*
there followed a very different work: *Les Rêveries du promeneur solitaire* (*Reveries of the Solitary Walker*).

We are familiar with Rousseau's daily habit, continued during
his final years in Paris, of taking long afternoon walks into the
country. Alone now on earth, except for Thérèse, broken with
most of his friends, Rousseau is resolved no longer to concern
himself with the fate of his works or his reputation with pos-
terity. Instead, he will write down the reveries which accompany his walks so that, rereading them, he can enjoy these
thoughts each time anew.

During the last two months, he says, a complete calm has
been reestablished in his heart. Once more, not altogether
accurately, he evokes Montaigne, insisting that Montaigne wrote
his *Essays* for others. This became true only with the final
edition. Rousseau declares he is writing his *Rêveries* only for
himself. Let his enemies enjoy their attacks on him, he will be
content with his innocence and will finish his days in peace. This
is the end of the *First Walk*, which is purely introductory.

The *Second Walk* is less general, more detailed. On Thurs-

day, October 24, 1776, relates Rousseau, after his noonday dinner, he was following the Boulevards as far as the Rue du
Chemin Vert by which one comes to the heights of Menil-
Montant and from there, through the open fields and vineyards,
he went as far as Charonne through the smiling countryside
which separates these two villages. Then he took a detour in
order to come back through these same fields by another way.
Here he observed with pleasure various botanical specimens,
some still in flower. Then, turning from the detailed to the
general, he noted that the harvesting of the grapes was finished
and the peasants were leaving the fields for their winter's
work. This thought of falling leaves and coming winter evoked
his own state of solitude and decline. "I was made to live," he
thought, "and I am dying without having lived."

Toward six o'clock, he was going down the slope toward
Menil-Montant when suddenly he saw a dog, a Great Dane,
and a carriage bearing down upon him. He tried to dodge, but
the huge dog knocked his legs from under him and he fell heavily,
unconscious.

It was almost night when he regained consciousness. Someone
asked who he was, and where he lived, and advised him to take
a cab. But, feeling chilled from lack of circulation, he preferred
to walk, made his way successfully to his apartment, Rue Plâtrière, climbed the five stairs in the dark, and appeared all
bloody to the horrified eyes of Thérèse.

M. Lenoir, Lieutenant General of Police, sent to inquire
if he could be of service to him. Rousseau, always suspicious,
made no reply. A Mme d'Ormoy tried to use his name in support
of a novel she was publishing. Jean-Jacques wrote her brusquely,
begging her "not to honor him further with her visits."

Rousseau hears that his death has been reported and a sub-
scription is being raised to publish his manuscripts. Further matter for suspicion and the *Second Walk* ends on that note.

The *Third Walk* opens with a brief quotation from Amyot's
translation of Plutarch: "I grow old, but continue to learn." The
task of an old man is to learn how to die. This passage again is
repeated by Montaigne, but is so well known that the latter
is not named.

References follow to Rousseau's period of Catholicism, his

admiration for Fénelon, and his associations with modern philosophers, who are destructive, unlike the philosophers of antiquity, builders of faith. We are reminded of his writing the *Savoyard Vicar* in *Emile* and of his new simplified Christianity, all a familiar story to us now. The *Third Walk* ends with further emphasis on how one can leave life better and more virtuous than at birth.

The *Fourth Walk* begins with another maxim of Plutarch: *How to profit from one's enemies.* Rousseau reflects on the lie he told in regard to poor Marion and the ribbon as narrated in the *Confessions.* Yet he has recounted many things of his own invention, while keeping a clear conscience and a love of truth. His addition of such passages to the *Confessions* is not in accordance with his motto and remains, he now believes, inexcusable. Once more, he emphasizes at the end, it is never too late to learn from one's enemies.

The *Fifth Walk* is particularly notable. "I have always passionately loved the water," Rousseau had written in the *Confessions,* "and the sight of it casts me into a delightful revery" (I, 642). He next narrates his happy sojourn in 1768 on the Island of Saint-Pierre in the middle of Lake Bienne near Neuchâtel.

"The banks of Lake Bienne are wilder and more *romantic* than those of Lake Geneva," writes Rousseau (using a word destined to give its name to a great literary movement), "because the rocks and woods come down closer to the water, but they are no less smiling."

In this tiny lake, little known or frequented at the time, Jean-Jacques enjoyed the charms of solitude and contemplation, taking refuge, after being stoned by mysterious enemies at Môtiers, in the single house located on one of these small islands. Here he was able to remain for only two months, "but I could have spent two years, two centuries, or a whole eternity without being bored a moment," exclaims Rousseau in dithyrambic exaggeration. After the emotional strains of recent years and the long period of intense literary activity, Rousseau's tired mind was glad to slip gently into the *dolce far niente* of these weeks of peaceful idling. His books and most of his other possessions reposed quietly in their packing cases, undisturbed, unwanted. Instead of occupying himself with his "gloomy papers," he says, he gave his time to the first fever of botanizing which filled his later years with purposeful tramps over the hills and countryside.

"When evening drew near, I descended the island slopes," wrote Rousseau,

and sat down happily on the shore of the lake. There the sound of the waves and the moving water, fixing my attention and driving all agitation from my spirit, plunged it into a delightful revery in which night often surprised me without my noticing it. The ebb and flow of the water, its continuous noise, swelling louder at intervals, ceaselessly striking my ear and my eyes, took the place of the inner movements effaced by the revery and sufficed to make me feel my existence with pleasure, but without the trouble of thought. From time to time there came a feeble and brief reflection on the instability of the things of this world represented by the image of the water's surface, but soon these slight impressions disappeared in the uniformity of the continuous movement by which I was lulled and which, without any active participation of my mind, did not fail to attract me until, summoned by the lateness of the hour and by the signal agreed upon, I could not tear myself away without effort.

The *Sixth Walk* contributes to a knowledge of certain psychological traits of Rousseau. It is in this respect an amplification of the *Confessions*. Up to the age of forty, he says, he remained the most trusting of men. He was never deceived. Now, he concludes, he was not made for society. He has not done much good for mankind, it is true, but he doubts if anyone has done less evil.

The *Seventh Walk* dwells on his interest in botany. An old man now, he has sometimes thought rather deeply, but never with pleasure. He has esteemed certain doctors, but never medicine in general. As was seen when he was with Mme de Warens, the *Confessions* tell us, he does not like to concern himself with the supposed medicinal properties of plants, but botany remains for him a pure amusement. It was a pleasure for him merely to recognize the different plants and then to understand their many individual characteristics.

The *Eighth Walk* asks the question: what does Rousseau need to make him happy? He does not know. He only knows when he is not happy. When his feelings do not work on his physical manifestations, he is the happiest of mortals. The moment he escapes from the company of mankind and enters a forest beneath the trees, he is the happiest of men. When the wind of passion ceases to blow, he is calm and happy. It is his ardent nature which causes his agitation. On the other hand, his indolence gives him peace.

The *Ninth Walk* shows his enjoyment now of children who seem in turn to find pleasure with him. One day he and Thérèse, walking in the Bois de Boulogne, meet a group of some twenty children conducted by a nun. A man appears, playing on a trumpet. It is a signal of the wafers he has for sale. The children want to buy his wafers. Rousseau pays for them all. At his request, the nun joins in too with the children. Rousseau was never happier.

One of the places in Paris that Rousseau especially liked to frequent was the vicinity of the Invalides where he could talk with the old soldiers. When they learned, however, that he was Rousseau, they were no longer friendly, but showed their hatred. They had surely been misled by rumors about him and his supposedly radical ideas. One old soldier, an "Invalide," embarked in a boat on the Seine at a time when the water of the river was rather rough. Rousseau paid his fare and the man did not refuse. Rousseau was sure the soldier had just come to Paris from the provinces and was still untouched by current gossip. Jean-Jacques longed to give him twenty-four cents to buy snuff, but, fearing a refusal, refrained.

The *Tenth Walk* opens strikingly: "Today, Palm Sunday, 12 April 1778, it is exactly fifty years since the beginning of my acquaintance with Mme de Warens." This had taken place on Palm Sunday, March 21, 1728. "She was then twenty-eight, being born with the century." It was so she must have told him, though she was really a year older at twenty-nine, being born in 1699. "I was not yet seventeen," continued Rousseau. "If it was not surprising that she should have conceived a liking for a young man active, but gentle and modest and of rather attractive features, it was still less so that a charming woman, intelligent and graceful, should have evoked my gratitude and also more tender feelings which I did not myself recognize."

Mme de Warens it was, who inspired him to read and study during those leisurely years at Les Charmettes. He enjoyed them because he did "only what I wanted to do," as he said. So it was that he acquired "a taste for solitude and reflection." It was there that he made up his mind to develop such talents as he might possess "and repay this best of women for the assistance she gave him."

Here the *Tenth Walk* suddenly stops. It was never finished. It remained in a chaotic first draft scribbled on playing cards like *Walks Eight* and *Nine* which preceded it, all equally difficult to decipher today. Evidently Rousseau himself tired of writing more, preferring the freedom of his early morning walks and botanizing at Ermenonville. But, with the *Tenth Walk* at any rate, there is a kind of poetic justice that the last words he wrote should have been this unalloyed tribute to the woman who had rescued him from failure and vagabondage and set him on his way. It would have been easy to have said too much and have spoiled the narrative.

For a time Rousseau continued to live in Paris in the busy Rue Plâtrière in his two-room apartment on the fifth floor where his new-found friend, Bernardin de Saint-Pierre, visited him, missing his count of the stairs in the obscurity by one flight in a very natural preoccupation with other thoughts and conversation with the great man. Later Rousseau and Thérèse moved to an apartment slightly lower on the fourth floor of the same building. Traffic was heavy on this street across from the Post Office, as J. S. Spink has shown (*Rêveries, op. cit.*, pp. I–III), and Rousseau was always happy when he had left the city's noisy congestion behind him and entered the pleasant open country beyond.

III *Ermenonville (1778)*

Finally, however, Rousseau accepted the invitation of the Marquis de Girardin on May 20 to take lodgings in his attractive private grounds at Ermenonville, some distance northeast of Paris. Finding the place, after a journey of exploration, much to his liking, he sent word for Thérèse to pack up and join him, spending the last six weeks of his life very pleasantly there.

Rising every morning by five o'clock, as he liked to do, Rousseau went for a vigorous walk or botanized in the park. Sometimes he was accompanied by a young son of the Marquis de Girardin, Jean-Jacques entertaining the boy by telling stories or showing him interesting characteristics of the grasses or herbs encountered on their way. At other times, a "freshwater admiral," as he enjoyed calling himself, he propelled a rowboat in a random course about the small lake or, stretched out flat in the bottom of the boat, drank in the immensity of the sky above him and gave himself over to agreeable revery. Evenings he played accompaniments on the Marquis's piano-forte while singing in his weak, cracked voice the song of the willows which he had himself composed after reading Shakespeare's *Othello* in the Letourneur translation, so violently castigated by Voltaire in a letter read before the French Academy by d'Alembert when the translation had first appeared two years before. At other times, Rousseau sang pieces by Gluck. It was all very pleasant, informal, and homelike.

When Voltaire toward the end of March was fêted at the Comédie-Française in Paris, some smart aleck thought to curry favor with Rousseau by attacking Voltaire as his enemy. "And why should Voltaire not be honored on the stage of which he is the master?" demanded Rousseau with open-minded realism, always ready to recognize Voltaire's varied gifts in spite of his enmity. Previously, Rousseau had subscribed two louis, a large sum for his limited exchequer, for a statue in honor of Voltaire. The latter, struck to the quick by this undesired favor, sought to prevent it on the grounds that Jean-Jacques, a native of Geneva, was a "foreign" author in Paris. It is not known whether Rousseau's broad-minded gift was accepted or not. The background on Voltaire's part becomes clear when it is recalled that at the time Rousseau's death was reported due to his being painfully struck down by the Great Dane as narrated in the *Second Walk* of the *Reveries*, Voltaire had written harshly to d'Alembert: "Jean-Jacques has done well to die!"

But when Voltaire in his eighty-fourth year died on May 30 in Paris, Rousseau could not fail to be moved as he heard the news a few miles away at Ermenonville. One of the great figures of eighteenth-century life had passed from the scene and Rousseau recognized it wholeheartedly.

On July 2, 1778, Rousseau set out early for his usual walk in the park, but he returned in a short time very ill ("fortement incommodé," I, lxxv), tried to take his usual light breakfast of coffee with milk and collapsed. With great difficulty Thérèse lifted him from the floor and stretched him out on his bed where he died at about eleven o'clock that morning. He was sixty-six years and four days old.

The following day the famous sculptor Houdon took a death mask, making possible later a statue which Rousseau had always previously opposed. Two days after his death, he was buried at eleven o'clock at night on the Island of Poplars at Ermenonville.

On October 11, 1794, Rousseau's remains were transferred to the Pantheon in Paris where those of Voltaire had been deposited in 1791.

CHAPTER 6

Conclusion

EARLY in life Rousseau showed an interest in writing. While in Turin as a rather privileged lackey of Mme de Vercellis during the later months of 1728, he had the good fortune to be chosen during her illness to take down letters at her dictation; and he quite naturally wrote letters on his own account to Mme de Warens at her home in Savoy. Living though she was in Italian Turin, Mme de Vercellis dictated her letters in an excellent French, not unworthy at times, observed Rousseau, of those by the famous Mme de Sévigné (I, 81). After the death of Mme de Vercellis, the good Abbé de Gouvon taught Jean-Jacques to read more thoughtfully and also had him continue the useful practice of writing from dictation. He was still only sixteen years old.

Back in Annecy probably no earlier than June, 1729, the boy Rousseau little by little developed superiority as a writer over his mentor, Mme de Warens, who consequently entrusted him with the composition of important letters and documents in her behalf. There followed on his own initiative significant autobiographical poems: *The Orchard of Mme de Warens* (1739), the *Epistle to M. Borde* (1741), and the *Epistle to M. Parisot* (1742). In 1740 he had written a *Project for the Education of M. de Sainte-Marie*, which he submitted to the young boy's father, M. de Mably, at Lyons. In Paris, Rousseau offered in writing an explanation of his proposed numerical signs for music during this same busy 1742. Several subjects for light plays drew his interest. There were: *The Prisoners of War, Harlequin in Love in Spite of Himself, The Bold Engagement,* and *Narcissus, or the Man in Love with Himself.* There was even a musical play, *Les Muses Gallantes* (*The Muses in Love*), which was so harshly criticized by the unfriendly composer Rameau that Rousseau felt it wise to have it dropped from the Opera. *Nar-*

124

cissus, however, had a very special appeal to him. Over a period of years Jean-Jacques worked on it persistently, revising and revising until at last in December, 1752, he had the rare pleasure of seeing it with a good cast brought on the stage of the august Comédie-Française. But alas! to his surprise, he found his one-act play so boring even to himself, the author, that, at the nearby Café Procope, he publicly with an unaccustomed frankness demanded its withdrawal. This was done after only two performances. No doubt, utter weariness from toiling over the lines repeatedly during these successive years had made him unable to grant the little play a chance for even the moderate success it might nevertheless have achieved.

Not one of these determined efforts had won him the fame he sought. They had, notwithstanding, their importance. They broadened his vocabulary, taught him problems of prose, poetry, and dialogue, led him to try out his talents in various literary forms, proving finally that they were not for his particular cast of mind. It is in these early years too, not as has formerly been supposed in 1750, that Rousseau made his first contact with that long-time inspiration of his attempts at verse and drama, the famous M. de Voltaire. Rousseau saw his idol only at a distance, it is true, when he appeared with other noted men and women at Mme Dupin's in April of 1743. Then, in December, 1745, Jean-Jacques initiated a respectful exchange of letters over adapting Voltaire's words to Rameau's music for production before the royal court. This last was all heady experience for the obscure, ambitious, but no longer young man that Rousseau by this time chanced to be.

With the astonishing success of his First Discourse in January, 1751, and the months following during the next two to three years, Rousseau, thanks to the Academy of Dijon, found himself near the age of forty at last belatedly on his way. He set himself to personal reform, started to live the simpler life he had preached so fervently in his First Discourse. Man is naturally good, he thought, not condemned to be the helpless victim of a theological Fall. By taking thought in a constructive way, man has it in his power to reorganize society with less of the appalling inequality which now exists between individuals and with more justice in other respects. This is the lesson of the Second

Discourse, of the *Nouvelle Héloïse*, the teaching of *Emile*. Suggestive of better government though it is, Rousseau did not fully solve the problem of political freedom in his *Social Contract*. His unfortunate obsession with a civil religion, not necessarily to be believed in detail, yet enforceable as a guarantor of obedience to the laws under pain of banishment or even death, stood ominously in the way. Later, Rousseau came to admit that his *Social Contract* needed to be rewritten. Whether he knew exactly what it lacked, he did not make clear. At any rate, he approached in some ways nearer to democracy in his *Letters from the Mountain*.

Rousseau is notably an apostle of the inner life. A dialogue with himself constantly occupies his thoughts. This communion with himself is one of the reasons why his *Confessions* prove so absorbing to the reader. In them, we witness the author's slow rise from sad beginnings, his gradual progress in moral ideas, in spite of neglect by father and uncle, the loss of a mother's care, the first sordid milieu of the Spirito Santo in Turin. Rousseau's inner life continues to be reflected, even if in part pathologically, in those half-mad *Dialogues: Rousseau Judge of Jean-Jacques*. Finally, Rousseau's life of the mind and the emotions manifests itself strikingly and in varied form in his concluding work, the *Reveries of the Solitary Walker*, ending with the unfinished tribute to Mme de Warens.

Rousseau's inner life was especially favorable to his religion. Largely free of dogma through his intimacy with the *philosophes*, his religious feeling remained independent and intensely personal. He held firmly to belief in God, in Providence, and in the rewards of a future life, while shocking both Catholics and Protestants by rejecting eternal damnation of the wicked, miracles, and a divine revelation. He had great respect for the Gospels and for the life of Christ. His *Letter to M. de Beaumont, Archbishop of Paris*, makes evident his religious views.

Although Rousseau had a clear feeling that revolution of some kind was in the air, he was at heart, in spite of the boldness of his ideas, the least revolutionary of men. He has often been described as having daring premises followed by cautious conclusions. Like his philosophic contemporaries, he did not realize to how great a degree his sharp questioning of existing institutions could prove unsettling to society in the future. His *Social Contract*, as Daniel Mornet has shown, appears to have been comparatively neglected in France until the eve of the Revolution. Then it began to attract much attention and to turn people's thoughts toward the basic obligation on the part of rulers to provide good government for their people, a principle at the heart of Rousseau's political thought. His emphasis on the value of national outdoor festivals repeated itself in Robespierre's inauguration of public tribute to the Supreme Being, but Rousseau, like Voltaire and the *philosophes* in general, would have recoiled in horror from the revolutionary Terror. It was not in this sanguinary way that he sought or expected the reform of society.

There exists an important area, however, where Rousseau's influence remained completely peaceful. His vivid depiction of scenes in Switzerland, in the forest about him in Montmorency, his personal emotion and feeling, his intensity of religious belief, all reappeared in some degree among successors like Bernardin de Saint-Pierre, Chateaubriand, Mme de Staël, Hugo, Vigny, Lamartine, and Musset, the great French Romantics. Byron, Wordsworth, Coleridge, and others in England, Lessing, Schiller, Goethe, and the philosopher Kant in Germany, owe a debt to Rousseau, while still remaining individuals. None of them imitated Rousseau slavishly. Each in fact made also his own independent contribution to the form and content of literature. But certainly they, and others of the realistic and naturalist schools, would have been different if Rousseau's powerful, original imagination had not loomed up before them, pointing out the way. Reason, emotion, and a vivid picture of the outside world are in Rousseau commingled in unusual proportions, making of him a giant figure in world literature.

Notes and References

Unless otherwise indicated passages cited within the body of the book are taken from the *Confessions*.

Chapter One

1. D'Alembert, *Mélanges de littérature, d'histoire et de philosophie*, II (Amsterdam: Chatelain, 1766), p. 372: "Des Loix somptuaires défendent l'usage des pierreries et de la dorure, limite[nt] la dépense des funérailles, et obligent tous les Citoyens à aller à pié dans les rues; on n'a de voitures que pour la campagne." This law was no doubt subject to exception also for private vehicles carrying heavy loads.
2. *Encyclopaedia Britannica*, 10th ed., XI (New York: 1911), p. 587. Art. *Geneva, Hist.*
3. D'Alembert, *op. cit.*, II. p. 369.
4. Mlle Galley was twenty years old, Mlle de Graffenried seventeen, and Rousseau eighteen.
5. Cf. L. Grünberg, "J.-J. Rousseau, joueur d'échecs," *Ann. J.-J. Rousseau*, III (1908), pp. 57–74.
6. Information by letter through the courtesy of Professor English Showalter, Jr., editor of the letters of Mme de Graffigny.
7. Contrary to Rousseau's opinion in the *Confessions* (I, p. 338 and n. 3), Voltaire's name also did not appear in the program.

Chapter Two

1. For further information about Rousseau's First Discourse, see my critical edition, J.-J. Rousseau, *Discours sur les sciences et les arts*, New York, Modern Language Association of America, 1946; Krauss reprint, 1966.
2. Montaigne, *Œuvres complètes*, Pléiade ed., Paris, Gallimard, 1962. Essai, *Du Pédantisme*, p. 142.
3. Rousseau, *Œuvres*, Nouvelle édition, Paris, Werdet et Lequien Fils, 1826, XIII, 226.
4. Montaigne, *op. cit.*, Essai, *Des Cannibales*, Pléiade ed., p. 212.
5. René Hubert, *Rousseau et l'Encyclopédie: Essai sur la formation des idées politiques de Rousseau*, Paris, Gamber, [1928], 25–26.

6. T. D. Kendrick, *The Lisbon Earthquake,* New York and Philadelphia, Lippincott. [1955 or 1956], p. 59. It has finally been estimated that from 10,000 to 15,000 people lost their lives as a result of the different phases of the earthquake.

Chapter Three

1. Rousseau, *Les Rêveries,* ed. by Marcel Raymond, Lille, Giard; Genève, Droz, 1948, p. 181.

2. G. Lanson, *Histoire de la littérature française,* 23rd ed., Paris, Hachette, n.d. [1922?], p. 789.

3. Rousseau, *Les Rêveries,* ed. by John S. Spink, Paris, Didier, 1948, p. vii. Thus Rousseau read this continuation of *Emile* to Bernardin de Saint-Pierre, visiting him in his apartment, Rue Plâtrière, and outlined to him one of the wild plots with which he hoped to complete it. Cf. also J. F. Hamilton, "Rousseau's Theological Oppression of Sophie," *Studi francesi,* 1974, pp. 478–80.

Chapter Four

1. ... "et un peu d'acquis." Cf. *Confessions* (I, p. 113): In the judgment of M. d'Aubonne, Rousseau says of himself: "J'étois, sinon tout à fait inepte, au moins un garçon de peu d'esprit, sans idées, *presque sans acquis,* très borné en un mot, à tous égards." This citation shows the meaning to be primarily one of mental attainment. The critical edition of the *Lettres à M. de Malesherbes* prepared by Gustave Rudler, London, Scholartis Press, 1928, naturally prints (p. 55): "et un peu d'argent," following the reading of Dufour-Plan, the chief edition available at that time before the work of R. A. Leigh.

Chapter Five

1. Later Rousseau admitted to Bernardin de Saint-Pierre that he had been too severe in condemning doctors and regretted it. Ed. Souriau, Cornély, 1907, p. 99.

Selected Bibliography

General Bibliographical Suggestions:

CABEEN, DAVID C. *A Critical Bibliography of French Literature.* Vol. IV: *The Eighteenth Century,* ed. by George R. Havens and Donald F. Bond. Syracuse University Press, 1951. Chap. VIII, *J.-J. Rousseau,* by Paul M. Spurlin.

————. *Ibid. The Eighteenth Century, Supplement,* ed. by Richard Brooks, Syracuse University Press, 1968. Chap. VIII, *J.-J. Rousseau,* by John W. Chapman.

GAY, PETER. *The Enlightenment, An Interpretation: The Rise of Modern Paganism.* New York, Knopf, 1966. Pp. 421–552: Extensive *Bibliographical Essay.* Lists many titles with each title evaluated, supplementing Cabeen.

Recent detailed bibliography of Rousseau in: *1975 MLA International Bibliography,* Vol. II, New York, MLA, 1977, pp. 30–31, nos. 1681–1752, plus supplementary numbers; Raymond Trousson, "Quinze années d'études rousseauistes," *Dix-Huitième Siècle,* IX, 342–86, 1977.

PRIMARY SOURCES

ALEMBERT, JEAN LE ROND D', Article *Genève* in *Encyclopédie,* Vol. VII, Paris, 1757, In *Mélanges de littérature, d'histoire et de philosophie,* Nouvelle édition, Amsterdam, Chatelain, 1766, Tome Second, pp. 357–86.

————. *Lettre à M. Rousseau, Citoyen de Genève, Ibid.,* pp. 387–454.

(On d'Alembert and Rousseau, cf. Martha V. Krauss, "Rousseau's *Lettre à d'Alembert sur les spectacles.*" Unpublished thesis for the degree of Master of Arts, Ohio State University, 1951. Much information on composition, plays seen by Rousseau, and general background.)

ROUSSEAU, J.-J. *Œuvres complètes,* Pléiade ed., Paris, Gallimard. Vol. I (1959), Vol. II (1961), Vol. III (1964), Vol. IV (1969). Vol. V (not yet published). Edition on thin paper with over 1,900 pp. per volume. Excellent introductions and copious notes.

Indispensable. Ed. by Bernard Gagnebin and Marcel Raymond with the cooperation of other leading Rousseau scholars. Only Vol. II is not indexed, the *Nouvelle Héloïse* no doubt offering special difficulties.

——. *Correspondance générale,* ed. by Théophile Dufour and Pierre-Paul Plan. Paris, Armand Colin, 1924–34, 20 vols. *Table de la Corr. Générale,* by Pierre-Paul Plan, Genève, Droz, 1953.

——. *Correspondance complète,* ed. by R. A. Leigh. Genève, Les Délices, 1965 ff. (25 vols. pub. by 1977 out of an estimated total of about 40 vols. when complete). Excellent. Many newly-discovered or more accurate letters by or to Rousseau. Well annotated. Supersedes the previous edition of the *Correspondance* for the volumes so far published.

——. *Discours sur les sciences et les arts,* édition critique by George R. Havens. New York, Modern Language Association of America, 1946; Kraus reprint, New York, 1966.

——. *Du Contrat social.* Ed. by C. E. Vaughan. Manchester University Press, London; New York, Longmans, Green, 1918. Authoritative edition.

——. *Lettre à d'Alembert sur les spectacles,* éd. critique par M. Fuchs. Textes littéraires français. Lille, Giard; Genève, Droz, 1948.

——. *Ibid.* In J.-J. Rousseau, *Œuvres,* Nouvelle édition, par Mussay Pathay, Paris, Werdet et Lequien Fils, 1826, Vol. XI, pp. 3–187.

——. *La Nouvelle Héloïse,* ed. by Daniel Mornet, 4 vols. Paris, Hachette, 1925. Detailed notes, extensive introduction. Authoritative.

——. *Les Rêveries du Promeneur solitaire,* ed. by Marcel Raymond. Lille, Giard; Genève, Droz, 1948.

——. *Les Rêveries du Promeneur solitaire,* ed. by John S. Spink, Paris, Marcel Didier, 1948.

VOLTAIRE, FRANÇOIS-MARIE AROUET DE. *Correspondence,* Definitive Edition by Theodore Besterman. 51 vols. Vol. I, Geneva, 1968; final vol., Oxford, 1977. Corresponds to the *Complete Works of Voltaire,* Vols. 85–135.

SECONDARY SOURCES

BERNARDIN DE SAINT-PIERRE, *La Vie et les ouvrages de J.-J. Rousseau,* édition critique par Maurice Souriau. Paris, Edouard Cornély, 1907.

CASSIRER, ERNST. *The Question of J.-J. Rousseau.* Translated and edited by Peter Gay. Indiana University Press, 1963. (First published, 1954). Basic first-hand study of Rousseau's thought.

COURTOIS, LOUIS J. *Chronologie critique de la vie et des œuvres de J.-J. Rousseau.* In *Ann. J.-J. Rousseau,* XV, 1923. Reprinted, Genève, Jullien, 1924. Indispensable basic study, occasionally superseded by later research of other scholars.

CROCKER, LESTER G. *J.-J. Rousseau: The Quest (1712–1758).* New York, Macmillan, Vol. I, 1968; *J.-J. Rousseau: The Prophetic Voice (1758–1778).* Vol. II, New York, Macmillan, 1973. Carefully prepared detailed study with emphasis on the dangers the author sees in Rousseau's ideas. Extensive bibliography divided between the two volumes.

DERATHÉ, ROBERT. *Le Rationalisme de J.-J. Rousseau.* Paris, Presses universitaires, 1948. Thorough study of role of reason in Rousseau's thought.

DUCROS, LOUIS. *J.-J. Rousseau.* Vol. I, *De Genève à l'Hermitage (1712–1757).* Paris, Fontemoing, 1908; Vol. II, *De Montmorency au Val de Travers (1757–1765),* Paris, Boccard, 1917; Vol. III, *De l'Ile de Saint-Pierre à Ermenonville (1765–1778).* Paris, Boccard, 1918. Thorough, impartial. Bibliography by chapters.

ELLIS, MADELEINE B. *Julie or La Nouvelle Héloïse: a Synthesis of Rousseau's Thought (1748–1759).* University of Toronto Press, 1949. Useful study whose main tendency is indicated by the title.

————. *Rousseau's Socratic Aemilian Myths: A Literary Collation of "Emile" and the "Social Contract."* Ohio State University Press, 1977. A challenging figurative Socratic and Biblical interpretation of these two works running parallel with the literal meaning. Does not mention Rousseau's unconscious threat to tolerance in his imposition of a "civil religion." Should we see in Rousseau's emotional reading to Kirchberger of his brief sequel, *Emile and Sophie, or the Solitaries,* an insistence on a literal interpretation of his moving story of seduction, grief, and voluntary exile?

Encyclopaedia Britannica. 10th ed., Vol. XI, New York, 1911. Article *Geneva,* History.

————. Chicago, 1968. Article *J.-J. Rousseau,* by John Plamenatz.

FOSTER, ELIZABETH A. *Le dernier Séjour de J.-J. Rousseau à Paris (1770–1778).* Smith College Studies, Northampton, Mass., 1921. Excellent study of the years indicated.

GAY, PETER. *The Party of Humanity: Essays in the French En-*

lightenment. New York, Knopf, 1964. Special study of the literature and questions about Rousseau, pp. 211–68.

GREEN, FREDERICK C. *J.-J. Rousseau: A Critical Study of His Life and Writings*. Cambridge University Press, 1955. Good study by well informed English scholar. Least successful in dealing with Rousseau's political ideas.

GRIMSLEY, RONALD. *J.-J. Rousseau: A Study in Self-Awareness*. Cardiff, University of Wales Press, 1961. Emphasis on Rousseau's personality viewed from the standpoint of modern psychology.

GROETHUYSEN, BERNHARD. *J.-J. Rousseau*. Paris, Gallimard. 1949. Excellent study of Rousseau's thought.

GRÜNBERG, L. "J.-J. Rousseau, joueur d'échecs." In *Ann. J.-J. Rousseau*, III, 57–74.

GUÉHENNO, JEAN. *Jean-Jacques: Histoire d'une conscience*. Nouvelle édition, Paris, Gallimard, 1962. 2 vols. Sympathetic and penetrating. Well written.

HAMILTON, JAMES F. "Rousseau's Theological Oppression of Sophie." In *Studi francesi*, 1974, 478–80.

HAVENS, GEORGE R. *The Age of Ideas: From Reaction to Revolution in Eighteenth-Century France*. New York, Holt, 1955. Illustrated. Also in paperback without illustrations: New York, The Free Press, a branch of Macmillan, 1963. Four chapters on Rousseau, Chapters XIV–XVII (pp. 221–76), written for the general reader as well as for the scholar. Notes in the back in support of the details in the text.

————. *Voltaire's Marginalia on the Pages of Rousseau*. Ohio State University, Columbus, Ohio, 1933. Sharply contrasting views of the two men.

HENDEL, CHARLES W. *J.-J. Rousseau, Moralist*. London and New York, Oxford University Press, 1934. 2 vols. Penetrating study of Rousseau's thought with emphasis on Platonic background.

HUBERT, RENÉ. *Rousseau et l'Encyclopédie: Essai sur les idées politiques de Rousseau*. Paris, Gamber [1928]. Brief, but objective and very informative study.

KENDRICK, T. D. *The Lisbon Earthquake*. New York and Philadelphia, Lippincott [1955 or 1956]. Detailed account of the disaster with the discussions and sermons resulting from it. Voltaire's role. Estimates 10,000 to 15,000 perished.

LANSON, GUSTAVE. *Histoire de la littérature française*. 23rd ed., Paris, Hachette [1922?]. Excellent and detailed discussion of Rousseau, pp. 773–803. See Index for other references. Broadened views often indicated in parenthesis. Appreciative both of Rousseau and of Voltaire. "Il n'est pas nécessaire que leur guerre se continue dans nos esprits." (p. 792, n.)

————. "L'unité de la pensée de J.-J. Rousseau," *Ann. J.-J. Rousseau,* VIII, 1–31, 1912. Indispensable, basic study.

MASSON, PIERRE-MAURICE. *La Religion de J.-J. Rousseau.* 2nd ed. Paris, Hachette, 1916, 3 vols. Thorough study of Rousseau's religion throughout his works and also his influence.

MONTAIGNE, MICHEL DE. *Œuvres complètes,* Pléiade ed., Paris, Gallimard, 1962. Thin paper edition. Strangely deficient in failing to note great influence of Montaigne on Rousseau.

MORNET, DANIEL. *Rousseau l'homme et l'œuvre.* Paris, Boivin, 1950. Excellent brief study, well informed, objective. Notes the influence of the *Social Contract* in France largely delayed until the French Revolution. By the same author, see also his comprehensive edition of *La Nouvelle Héloïse.*

SPURLIN, PAUL M. *Rousseau in America.* University of Alabama Press, Athens, Ala., 1969. Based on thorough study of Colonial history, magazines, newspapers, book catalogues, letters, and other original sources. Finds no conclusive evidence of Rousseau's political influence on Jefferson or in general on America. Rousseau did influence America in education and in the novel.

STAROBINSKI, JEAN. *J.-J. Rousseau: la transparence et l'obstacle.* Paris, Plon, 1957. Emphasis on Rousseau's desire for "la transparence des cœurs" (p. 102), yet he is conscious of great obstacles. "Et l'on découvre, en lisant la sixième *Rêverie,* que l'obstacle le plus redoutable, le plus immobilisant, n'est autre que cette fausse image de Jean-Jacques qui se forme dans les consciences étrangères et qui lui dénie sa transparence." (p. 318).

VOLTAIRE, FRANÇOIS-MARIE AROUET DE. *Œuvres complètes,* Moland ed., Paris, Garnier, 1877–85, 52 vols. Confusingly, editor's name does not appear on the title page. Superseded for certain individual works by several excellent critical editions and for the *Correspondance* by the Besterman Definitive edition. A completely new edition of all the Voltaire Works awaits publication at Oxford, England.

WRIGHT, ERNEST H. *The Meaning of Rousseau.* Oxford University Press, Milford, 1929. Brief and compact. Excellent study of Rousseau's real meaning when he spoke of "la bonté naturelle."

Index

137